Henrik Ibsen
A DOLL'S HOUSE

a new adaptation
by Bryony Lavery

from a literal translation
by Neil Howard and Tonje Gotschalken

First published in this adaptation in 2004 by Oberon Books Ltd.
(incorporating Absolute Classics)
521 Caledonian Road, London N7 9RH
Tel: 020 7607 3637 / Fax: 020 7607 3629
e-mail: oberon.books@btinternet.com
www.oberonbooks.com

A catalogue record for this book is available from the British
Library.

ISBN: 1 84002 432 1

Cover design: Andrzej Klimowski

Printed in Great Britain by Antony Rowe Ltd, Chippenham.

Characters

NORA

HELMER

HELENE

MRS LINDE

ANNE-MARIE

DR RANK

KROGSTAD

CHILDREN

DELIVERY MAN

A Doll's House was first performed at the Birmingham REP on 3 February 2004, with the following cast:

NORA, Tara Fitzgerald

HELMER, Tom Goodman-Hill

MRS LINDE, Jane Gurnett

ANNE-MARIE, Pera Markham

DR RANK, Peter Guinness

KROGSTAD, Richard Clothier

HELENE, Masie Dimbleby

DELIVERY MAN, Will Gregson

Director, Rachel Kavanaugh

Designer, Ruari Murchison

Lighting Designer, Tim Mitchell

Composer, Terry Davies

ACT ONE

Christmas Eve

A comfortable, tasteful, but not expensively-furnished room. U.R. a door leading into the hall U.L. a door leading into HELMER's home office. Between them, a good piano. In the middle of the left wall, a door, and further downstage, a window. Near this window, a round table with armchairs and a small sofa. Towards the back of the right wall another door and further downstage, a stoneware stove with two armchairs and a rocking chair around it. Between this door and the stove, a small table. Etchings on the walls. A whatnot displaying porcelain figures and small objets d'art. A small bookcase filled with expensively bound books. A carpet on the floor, a fire in the stove. It is a winter's day. A bell rings in the hall. We hear the front door open.

NORA enters her room humming cheerfully. She wears outdoor clothes and carries an impressive number of parcels, which she offloads on the table to the right.

Through the open door we see a DELIVERY MAN with a Christmas tree and a basket, which he hands over to HELENE, the HELENE who opened the door.

NORA: Hide the Christmas tree, Helene.
   The children mustn't see it till this evening
   When it's all decorated.

   She takes out her purse…

   How much…?

DELIVERY MAN: Fifty ore.

NORA: Here you are. (*A hundred.*)

   Hands him one crown…mimes.

7

No… Keep the change.

The DELIVERY MAN mimes profuse surprised thanks and goes off happily.

NORA, laughing, closes the door and takes off her outdoor clothes. She takes out of her pocket a bag of macaroons. She eats one. She eats another one, walking stealthily to her husband's door and listening outside.

Ah. He's 'Home.'

She moves to the table, R, humming.

HELMER: (*From his office.*) What's all that chirruping? Not that Nora-bird?

NORA: (*Busy opening parcels.*) Yes it is.

HELMER: Not that squirrel nut-gathering again?

NORA: Yes.

HELMER: When did that squirrel get back?

NORA: Just now.

She hides the macaroon bag in her pocket. Wipes her mouth.

Come out come out wherever you are,
Torvald and see what I bought.

HELMER: No Interruptions! Do Not Disturb!

His door opens. Pen in hand.

Did you say 'bought'? All these nuts?
Has that Nora-Bird been scattering
Money again?

NORA: Yes, but Torvald…
This year we really must go a little bit mad
…mustn't we…????
The first Christmas we don't need to be
Careful!

HELMER: But we can't be 'careless'.

NORA: Oh yes, Torvald, we can! Just a little!
Just a nut!
Who is getting a *large* salary?
Who is going to earn pots and pots of money?

HELMER: Me.
From the beginning of the new year.
And then three long cold hard months before
The *large* salary arrives!

NORA: Tut! We can borrow a little bit if we need to!

HELMER: Nora!

Takes her by the ear. A married joke.

The Nora-bird's caught recklessness again!
Visualise…
Today, I borrow a thousand crowns
Christmas week, you spend every one…
New year's eve…a roof tile plummets from the roof
Slices / through my brain…

NORA: (*Gagging him.*) Oh No!
You mustn't say such / dreadful things!

HELMER: Oh Yes I must!
Imagine it…
What then?

NORA: If anything so terrible happened…
It wouldn't matter if I had debts or not!

HELMER: And what about the men I'd borrowed from?

NORA: Them?
Who cares about Them?
They're strangers, aren't they?

HELMER: Nora. Nora. Oh *essence* of woman!
Be serious now. You know what I think.

9

No debt. No borrowing. Ever.
A home founded on loan and debt…
It's not   free
It's not   beautiful somehow
We've managed so bravely until now
We two
And there's such a short time left…
We won't give up now.

NORA goes towards the warmth of the stove.

NORA: As you wish, Torvald.

HELMER: (*Following.*) Oh no, the skylark mustn't
Drag her wing.
What? Is that the squirrel…
And her nut hoard?

Takes out his wallet…

Nora! What's this in here?

NORA: (*Spinning round.*) Money!

HELMER: So it is! (*Gives her some notes.*) I know
How many nuts a nest needs at Christmas!

NORA: (*Counting.*) Ten…twenty thirty forty.
Oh Torvald thank you. Thank you.
I'll make this last and last, Torvald.

HELMER: You really must.

NORA: Yes, I will. I will.
Come here so I can show you
Everything I bought.
Very cheaply!
Look   new clothes for Ivar
And then a sabre!
A horse *and* a trumpet! For Bob.
And here is a doll in its cot! For Emmy.

It's not much…but she'll have it in
Pieces by Boxing Day anyway!
This is material and headscarves for the
Maids.
Oh, old Anne-Marie / should have
Something better…!

HELMER: And what's in that parcel?

NORA: No, Torvald! You' mustn't see that till
This evening!

HELMER: The unbearable suspense!
Now what are you planning for yourself?
Well…my millionairess?

NORA: For me?
Nothing.
I don't want anything.

HELMER: Oh yes you do.
Tell me.
Something reasonable.
Something you would really like.

NORA: No. There's nothing.
Oh.
Yes.
Listen Torvald

HELMER: Now What?

NORA: (*Fumbles with his buttons, not looking at him.*)
If you want to give me something
You could /
You could

HELMER: Yes…I could what…?

NORA: You could give me money, Torvald.
Only as much as you think you can spare
Then sometime / I'll buy myself something with it

HELMER: Ah, Nora…really.

NORA: Please! Dear Torvald. Really.
　　Then I could wrap it in lovely gold paper
　　And hang it on the Christmas tree!
　　That would be fun, wouldn't it?

HELMER: What are those birds
　　that are always
　　squandering money called?

NORA: Money Bills.
　　The GooseSquander.
　　The 'More' Hen.
　　I know I know.
　　But let's do what I say, Torvald.
　　I'll have time to think about what I need most.
　　Isn't that sensible?
　　Isn't it? Yes?

　　HELMER smiles.

HELMER: Sensible? Oh yes…
　　if you held on to the money I gave you
　　if you really bought something for yourself
　　If it didn't just go on the house
　　and all sorts of bits and bobs
　　So this hand would have to delve into
　　This wallet / once again.

NORA: But Torvald…

HELMER: Irrefutable evidence, Nora darling!

　　He puts his arm round her waist.

　　The swift! Swift of name
　　Swift of money!
　　It's unbelievable /
　　How expensive it is to keep a…

NORA: Shame on you!
Unfair prosecuting!
I really do / save everything I can!

HELMER: (*Laughing.*) Yes, you do.
Everything you can.
But you absolutely cannot!

NORA: (*Hums and smiles quietly, contentedly.*)
If you only knew just how many expenses
We More Hens and Money Bills have,
Torvald.

HELMER: You're a strange small species. Just like your
Father. Ever on the lookout for money.
When you get it, it trickles straight through
Your fingers. Abracadabra! Magic!
It's in the blood!
Your Inheritance.
But that makes you my Nora!

NORA: I wish I were more like Papa.

HELMER: I wish you as you are
My sweet gold billed gannet!
Except for…something just occurs to me
You look so…
What's the word…?
Suspicious?

NORA: Suspicious?

HELMER: Indubitably.
Look me right in the eyes.

NORA: (*Looks.*) Well?

HELMER: (*Threatens with his finger.*) That Hummingbird
Shouldn't have hovered about town today.

NORA: How could any bird watcher think that?

HELMER: Flown into a pastry shop.

NORA: No, I didn't!

HELMER: Siphoned a little honey through its beak.

NORA: I absolutely didn't!

HELMER: Picked up a macaroon or two?

NORA: Torvald, I absolutely promise / you I didn't!

HELMER: Now now now
Of course, just my little joke…

NORA goes to the table right.

It never entered my head. You hate me eating
Macaroons.

HELMER: I know. And you promised, didn't you?

He goes over to her.

Darling, keep your little
Christmas secrets. All will be revealed
When The Christmas tree is Lit.

NORA: Did you invite Doctor Rank?

HELMER: No. Not necessary.
Goes without saying he eats with us.
Anyway, he'll call here this morning.
I'll make sure then.
I have ordered some really good wines.
You've no idea how much I'm
Looking forward to this evening

NORA: Me too!
And won't the children / have a wonderful time,
Torvald?

HELMER: It is so marvellous to know one has
A secure, safe position.

And amply off!
Isn't it?
Think about it! Marvellous!

NORA: Yes. Marvellous!

HELMER: Remember last Christmas? Three whole weeks
You locked away until after midnight...
Making ornaments for the tree...
And all those other surprises!
I've never been so bored in my life!

NORA: And I've never been so unbored!

HELMER: (*Smiling.*) But then it ended so badly,
Didn't / it Nora?

NORA: Don't tease me.
Who could have foreseen the cat!
Sneaking in
Claws! everything / in shreds!

HELMER: Of course you couldn't!
You wanted to delight us all
You did your best
That is the point.
Still, it's good the lean years are over...

NORA: Yes! It is wonderful! Marvellous!

HELMER: I don't need to sit alone and bored
You don't need to strain your eyes
And rip your lovely paws...

NORA: (*Clapping her hands.*) No, I don't! No more need,
Torvald! What a wonderful thought! Takes his arm
Now listen, Torvald...I'll tell you how I think
We should go on once Christmas is out of the way...

A bell rings in the hall.

Oh, the doorbell!

NORA tidies up automatically…

Someone calling.
How boring!

HELMER: I'm not at home to visitors.

HELENE: At the door Madame…there's a lady…
I don't know her…

NORA: Well…let her come in…

HELENE: (*To HELMER.*) …and then the doctor
Arrived at the same moment…

HELMER: Did he go into the study?

HELENE: Yes, Sir.

HELMER goes into his room.

HELENE shows in MRS LINDE. Exits, closing door.

MRS LINDE wears travel clothes. Speaks diffidently and slightly hesitant…

LINDE: Hello, Nora.

NORA: (*Uncertain.*) Hello…

LINDE: You don't recognise me, do you?

NORA: I'm sorry I'm afraid I don't
Wait a moment…Yes!…well I think…
(*Crying out.*) Of course! Kristine!
Is it really you?

LINDE: Yes its really me.

NORA: Kristine! To not recognise you!
How could I not…
(*Quietly.*) You've changed so much, Kristine.

LINDE: Of course I have! Its been nine…ten years…

NORA: Has it been that long? It must...yes it must be!
Can you believe it? I've been so happy these
Last eight years! So you've come back to town?
That long journey in winter!
How brave of you.

LINDE: I arrived this morning on the steamer.

NORA: To have some fun at Christmas!
Perfect! We'll all have such fun this Christmas!
Well, take your coat off!
You must be freezing!

Helps her.

There. Now let's sit by the stove.
No, in the armchair! I'll rock!

She claps MRS LINDE's hands.

Yes, you're looking more like the old you
It was just at first...you're paler
And perhaps a bit thinner?

LINDE: And older, Nora. 'Much much older.'

NORA: Not much much older. Not even much...
Just a tiny little bit...
(*Stops, serious.*) Oh, I'm so thoughtless,
Sitting chattering!
Dear good Kristine, please forgive me.

LINDE: Forgive you? Why?

NORA: Poor Kristine, you lost your husband.

LINDE: Three years ago.

NORA: And of course, I knew. I saw it in
The newspapers. Oh Kristine...
I meant and meant and meant to write
But I didn't. I just didn't.

LINDE: It's alright.

NORA: No, it's not, Kristine. I was hopeless.
  Oh you poor thing. You've had such trials.
  He didn't leave you anything…?

LINDE: No.

NORA: And no children?

LINDE: No.

NORA: Nothing at all then?

LINDE: Not even the minutest speck of grief.

  NORA stares at her disbelieving.

NORA: Kristine can that be possible?

  MRS LINDE smiles and strokes NORA's hair.

MRS LINDE: Sometimes. Oh yes.

NORA: So, Alone then. Quite Alone.
  How dreadful for you. I have
  Three lovely children. You can't see them
  Just yet. Nanny's taken them out.
  Now tell me all about it…

LINDE: No, you tell me all about it…

NORA: No, you start. I won't be selfish today.
  Today I want to think about you. Except
  For one thing…have you heard our great news?

LINDE: No. What is it?

NORA: My husband has been appointed
  Director of The Joint Stock Bank!

LINDE: Your husband? That's wonderful…

NORA: Yes, isn't it? Being a lawyer is so
  Precarious – especially when one (*Torvaldish.*) 'will

Not have to do with any case that's not
Above board and quite the thing'.
That's Torvald for you
And I absolutely take his view on this!
Oh, we are so excited!
On New Year's day he starts work at the bank
And he'll be receiving a large salary
With *bonuses*… From now on we can
Live properly.
Oh Kristine, the weight off my shoulders!
It is splendid to have oodles of money
And never have to worry again.
Isn't it?

LINDE: Yes. It must be lovely to have what you need.

NORA: Oh more than what you need. Oodles!

LINDE smiles.

LINDE: Nora Nora not learned sense yet?
Remember in school? You spending
Money like water!

NORA laughs quietly.

NORA: I know and Torvald says
I still do! wags her finger But 'Nora Nora' is
Not as silly as you suppose – We've not been in
Any position to be silly. We've both had to
Work.

LINDE: You too?

NORA: Me too. Bits and pieces. Crochet, embroidery,
Things like that and
(*Casual.*) Other things as well.
You know Torvald left the Civil Service
When we got married?
No promotion prospects in his office
And then he had to earn more money…

But the first year he overworked and
Pushed himself too hard
He had to take on every sort of extra work
You've no idea! Slaving from dawn to dusk.
It was too much for him
And he became so ill…
Then the doctors told me I
Had to take him South.

LINDE: You spent a year in Italy, didn't you?

NORA: Yes. It was a nightmare to arrange!
I'd just had Ivar. But, clearly, we had to go.
Oh it was a wonderful year. And it
Saved Torvald's life. And it cost a fortune,
Kristine.

LINDE: I'm sure it did.

NORA: Four thousand eight hundred crowns. *Four thousand
eight hundred crowns.*
That's a lot of money.

LINDE: How lucky you had it when you needed it.

NORA: We got it from Papa of course.

LINDE: Ah. It was around the time your father died.

NORA: Yes, Kristine, about then. And the awful thing
Was… I couldn't go and look after him. I was
Expecting Ivar any second…and I had my poor
very poorly Torvald to look after.
My dear kind Pappa! I never saw him again.
That's the heaviest blow
I've had since I married.

LINDE: I know how much he meant to you.
prompts so you went to Italy…?

NORA: Yes. We had the money. The doctors
Were saying 'hurry ! Quick!' So we left the next
Month…

LINDE: And your husband came back well?

NORA: As fit as a fish!

LINDE: But…then…why the doctor?

NORA: I'm sorry?

LINDE: I thought that your maid said it was the doctor…
The gentleman who arrived the same time as me…?

NORA: Doctor Rank, yes.
It's not a professional visit.
He's our best friend. He looks in at least once a day.
No, Torvald hasn't had a sick day since.
The children are fit as fish and I am too!

She jumps up and claps her hands.

Oh God, Kristine, it is so wonderful
To be alive and happy!
Oh, I am really too awful…drivelling
On about me me me!

*She sits down on a footstool close by MRS LINDE. Puts her
arms on MRS LINDE's knees…*

I forbid you to be angry with me!
Tell me…did you really not love your husband
At all? Why did you marry him? Tell me.

LINDE: My mother was still alive.
She was bedridden. Helpless.
And I had two younger brothers
To take care of. He MADE ME AN OFFER I COULDN'T
Refuse.

NORA: I see. Yes. So was he fabulously rich?

LINDE: He had money…but also…a precarious
Business. So when he died, the whole
Structure toppled. There was nothing left.

NORA: And then…?

LINDE: I managed a little shop.
    Then a little school.
    Then anything that turned up. The last three
    Years have been like one long interminable,
    Tea-breakless working day. But its over now. Nora.
    My poor mother doesn't need me because
    She's passed away… neither do the boys…
    They've got (*Son-speak.*) 'positions' and
    'can look after themselves'.

NORA: You must be so relieved…

LINDE: Empty. I'm unutterably empty.
    No-one to live for any more

She gets up restlessly.

    That's why I couldn't stand it
    Any more stuck out there in that wilderness
    It must be easier here to find something
    To fill my time and my head
    If only I could be lucky enough to
    Land a job…some office work…

NORA: Oh Kristine, No…you'll be exhausted and
    You look so tired already.
    Why don't you go to a spa…?

MRS LINDE goes to the window

LINDE: Nora, I don't have a Pappa to
    Give me money for holidays

NORA gets up.

Oh, don't be angry with me!

MRS LINDE goes over to her.

Don't *you* be angry with me, Nora.
In my position, you become bitter

Which is so soul-destroying!
No-one to work for
But on your toes every minute.
One must live, so one must become selfish.
Can you believe it...
When you told me your good news
I was happy for me, not you...

NORA: Why? Oh.
You think Torvald might be able
To help you...

LINDE: Yes.

NORA: Well, he will, Kristine
Leave it to me.
I shall weave in the idea when I've
Got him into a receptive frame of mind. /
Oh I so want to help you!

LINDE: This is so handsome of you
To watch out for me...
So kind when you know so little /
Of how hard life can be...

NORA: I...know so little...?

MRS LINDE smiles.

LINDE: Well... Good God, crochet, a bit of needle.
You're a child, Nora.

NORA tosses her head and walks across the floor.

NORA: You shouldn't put me down, Kristine

LINDE: Shouldn't I?

NORA: You're like everybody else.
You all think I wasn't built to do anything serious.

LINDE: Now now...

NORA: …that I haven't done anything in this difficult world…

LINDE: Nora, dear you've just told me all your troubles!

NORA: The little ones! (*Quietly.*) I haven't told you the Big one…

LINDE: What 'big one?'

NORA: You dismiss me utterly, Kristine. You mustn't.
You're proud you worked so long and so
Hard for your mother.

LINDE: I dismiss no-one.
It's true I'm proud and happy I could help my
Mother / in her last years.

NORA: And you're proud of what you have done
For your brothers.

LINDE: I think I have a right to be.

NORA: I think so too. But listen, Kristine
I've a right to be proud and happy too.

LINDE: Of course you have. What?

NORA: Quietly.
If Torvald heard this!
He must never hear this.
No one but you must know this, Kristine!

LINDE: Know what?

NORA: Come here.

She pulls MRS LINDE down onto the sofa.

Yes, I have something to
Be proud and happy about.
I saved Torvald's life. / I saved his life!

LINDE: Saved? How?

NORA: The year in Italy. Torvald would have
Died without that year in Italy.

LINDE: Well, yes, but your father gave you the
Money…

NORA: That's what Torvald thinks…that's what
Everybody thinks…but…

LINDE: But…

NORA: Pappa didn't give us one schilling.
I found the money.

LINDE: You found the money…all that money?

NORA: Four thousand eight hundred crowns!
How about that?

LINDE: How is that possible? You won the lottery!

NORA: (*Disdain.*) The lottery! Where's the skill in that?

LINDE: So where did you get it from?

NORA hums and smiles secretively.

You couldn't have borrowed it.

NORA: Oh? Why not?

LINDE: Well…
A wife can't borrow without her husband's consent.

NORA: What if the wife knows a thing or two about money?
What if the wife has a business brain?

LINDE: I'm confused.

NORA: Are you? Did I say I borrowed the money?

She throws herself on the sofa.

Perhaps I had
An admirer, a generous admirer…someone as
Attractive as me…

LINDE: You're mad.

NORA: And you're mad with curiosity, Kristine.

LINDE: Nora…dear…have you done something silly?

NORA sits again.

NORA: Silly? To save one's husband's life?

LINDE: I think it's silly to do something
    without his knowledge…

NORA: Absolutely without his knowledge!
    Dear God, that was the point!
    Don't you understand?
    He couldn't be told how ill he was.
    The doctors came to me.
    They said 'He's dangerously ill.
    You must take him south!'
    Don't you think I tried to persuade him?
    'Torvald, darling, I want to travel
    Abroad like other young wives!'
    I cried I begged
    I said 'remember my Condition!
    Be generous, darling, humour me.
    Spoil me!'
    I said 'perhaps you could take out a loan…'
    Then he nearly got angry, Kristine
    He said 'you're frivolous and irresponsible…
    It is my duty as your husband not
    To listen to your whims and moods'
    I think it was 'whims and moods'…
    I thought, you have to be saved, yes
    And I discovered the escape route…

LINDE: Your husband never found out?
    Your father didn't tell him?

NORA: Never. No. Because…Pappa died.
    I thought about telling him everything

And saying 'don't tell, Pappa' but he
Was lying there so ill...and then it
Was suddenly, unnecessary.

LINDE: And you never confessed to your husband /
Since...?

NORA: For heaven's sake, No! How could I?
He's very strict about money!
And Torvald's a man
It would be so embarrassing and
humiliating if he thought he owed me
Anything. It would quite disturb
What we have
It would upset our lovely happy home.

LINDE: Will you never tell him?

NORA half smiles, contemplative.

NORA: Yes one day maybe
Many Years From Now! When My Looks
Have Gone! Don't laugh...I mean...
Come on...there will come a time when
Torvald isn't quite so 'in love' with me...
Not quite so enthralled by my dancing
My dressing up
How I play...
Then it might be good to have something
Up my sleeve...

She breaks off...

Nonsense nonsense nonsense
That time will never come.
So, Kristine, what about My Secret?
I am Good for something, you see
And you must understand how anxious
This makes me...
How hard it is to fulfil obligations

On time…you see Kristine…it involves
In the business world…something called
'quarterly interest' and 'instalments'
And it is always a nightmare to manage them.
I had to skrimp a little here, save a little there…
I couldn't really put any housekeeping money aside…
Because Torvald has to live well,
and I couldn't let the children go out in rags!
Whatever I got for them I spent on them. Had to.
The littlies!

LINDE: So it was your needs that suffered, Nora?

NORA: Obviously. It was my responsibility, completely.
Whenever Torvald gave me dress and pin money
I never spent more than half
I always bought the minimum, the cheapest.
God's luck…everything looks well on me.
Torvald didn't notice.
But I did find that hard, Kristine…
It's so nice to be beautifully dressed…
Isn't it?

LINDE: Oh yes indeed.

NORA: I also had 'other sources of income'!
Last winter I landed a whole lot of copying!
I locked myself in every evening and
Wrote late into the night.
I was so tired, ah so so tired.
But it was tremendous fun too.
Sitting and earning money.
It was almost as if I were a man.

LINDE: How much have you paid off so far?

NORA: I'm not sure, exactly. It's a complicated…
Business to keep track of…I just
Know everything I've scraped together…I've
Paid it all out.

The times I've been at my wit's end! (Smiles.) then I'd sit
and dream.
'There was this rich man, this old rich man…
So in love with me…'

LINDE: What old rich man?

NORA: It was the Talk of The Town!
That now he was dead…and when
They read the will…there, in big letters
It said, 'All my money to be paid
Out to the amiable and charming
Mrs Nora Helmer. At Once. In Cash!'

LINDE: Nora…which old rich man????

NORA: Good God, can't you understand? No rich old man!
It was just something I sat here and
Conjured up when I couldn't conjure up
Any money! Well, he needn't die now!
Let him Live! Let him Change his Will
I don't need him now.

Jumps up.

Oh God, I'm free! It's so good, Kristine!
Carefree! Quite Free of Care
To be able to rough and tumble with the littlies!
To have a 'handsome beautiful house'
For Torvald!
And spring is coming with   big blue air!
We could travel again!
I could see the sea again!
It is wonderful to be alive.
Yes yes yes!

The bell is heard and MRS LINDE gets up.

LINDE: Visitors. I'd better go.

NORA: No, stay. I'm not expecting anyone.

It'll be someone for Torvald…

HELENE is in the doorway to the hall.

HELENE: Excuse me, madam, there's a gentleman
Wanting to speak to the lawyer…

NORA: The bank director, you mean.

HELENE: Yes, the bank director, but the doctor's still
there…

NORA: Who is the gentleman?

KROGSTAD is in the doorway to the hall.

KROGSTAD: It's me, madam.

MRS LINDE, astonished, starts and turns to the window.

NORA: (*A pace towards him, tense, in a low voice.*) You?
What is it? Why d'you want to talk to my husband.

KROGSTAD: Bank business you might say.
I do hold a junior post at the Joint Stock bank…
And now I hear your husband is to become our boss…

NORA: That is…

KROGSTAD: Just boring bank business, madam. Nothing
else.

NORA: Well then…
Be so good as to go through to his office.

*She nods indifferently as she closes the door to the hallway.
Then she goes to see to the stove.*

LINDE: Nora who was that man?

NORA: Just a lawyer. Mr Krogstad.

LINDE: It was really him then.

NORA: You know this person?

LINDE: I did years ago
    He was once a fully qualified solicitor /
    In my part of the world.

NORA: Yes that's what he was.

LINDE: How he's changed.

NORA: He was probably very unhappily married too.

LINDE: He's a widower now?

NORA: With loads of children. Look. It's
    Burning.

*She closes the stove door and moves the rocking chair slightly
to one side.*

LINDE: They say he dabbles in all sorts of business.

NORA: Do they? Yes. Maybe…but let's not
    Think about business…it's so boring…

*DR RANK enters from HELMER's office. He speaks in the
doorway.*

RANK: No no I won't disturb you.
    I'd much rather visit your wife!

Closes the door and notices MRS LINDE.

Oh, I beg your pardon
    I see I am disturbing someone here too!

NORA: No you're not. Doctor Rank. Mrs Linde.

RANK: So. A name which is often heard here
    In this house. I believe I passed you on the stairs…

LINDE: You did. Climbing slowly. I'm no good with stairs.

RANK: Aha underpowered?

LINDE: Actually overwork.

RANK: Overwork And you come on a rest cure
    Among all the Christmas parties?

LINDE: I've come to find work.

RANK: That being a cure for tiredness?

LINDE: One has to live, Doctor.

RANK: Has one? Is that the general prognosis?

NORA: Come on, Doctor Rank, you rather want to live.

RANK: As it happens, I rather do.
    Wretched as I am, please prolong the agony.
    All my patients concur.
    As do the mentally sick.
    Just such an example being at this moment
    In with Helmer…

LINDE: Ah.

NORA: What do you mean?

RANK: Krogstad. Lawyer. Scandal-Mongerer.
    Jack of All Trades
    A man beyond your Understanding.
    Going to The Bad Before Our Very Eyes
    Currently insisting,
    as a matter of priority, one must live.

NORA: What is he talking to Torvald about?

RANK: Not My field! Bank business!

NORA: I didn't know Krog…this lawyer Krogstad
    Had anything to do with the bank…

RANK: Works there, apparently. In some capacity.
    (*To LINDE.*) Mrs Linde, is it the practice
    Where you come from…to have the kind of
    Person who loves to scurry about sniffing
    Out Moral Decay…and then to say

'Let's put him in a rather good position
So we can keep an eye on him
As *most* of the stench seems to be coming from *him*!!'
Se *He's* admitted for observation
While the healthy and whole queue round the block?

LINDE: Well, surely the sick need the most healing.

RANK shrugs his shoulders.

Ah, there we have it.
So society turns itself into a general hospital.

NORA in her own thoughts laughs to herself, clapping.

RANK: You're laughing. Our Sick Society amuses you?

NORA: Who cares about boring society?
I was laughing about something else.
Very funny.
Tell me, Dr Rank, will all employees
of Joint Stock bank now be under Torvald's command?

RANK: You find that funny?

NORA: (*Smiles and hums.*) …That's my business.
Haha, my business!

Walks the floor

Yes, it is hilarious to think that we
That Torvald has so much influence over
So many people…

Takes a bag out of her pocket.

…Doctor Rank…will it be a little
Macaroon?

RANK: Look! Beware! Macaroons! Aren't they
Illegal here?

NORA: They are but Kristine Brought Them In.

33

LINDE: Me? What?

NORA: Settle down now. You weren't to know
     Torvald's declared them illegal.
     He's afraid I'll lose my teeth!
     But a little of what you fancy…
     Yes, Dr Rank?

Puts a macaroon in his mouth.

There you are. You too, Kristine.
     And one for me. A little one.
     Two. And that's it.

Walks about again.

Now there's only one thing in the world I
     Really really want.

RANK: What?

NORA: Something I tremendously need to say while
     Torvald's listening.

RANK: Why can't you say it?

NORA: I daren't. It's bad.

LINDE: Bad.

RANK: Then my diagnosis is don't.
     Say it to us. Better out than in.
     What do you need to say to Helmer?

NORA: I need to say   death and pain.

RANK: Ah. Dementia.

LINDE: Nora good gracious…

RANK: Say it. He's here.

NORA hides the macaroons.

NORA: Be quiet.

HELMER with overcoat over his arm, hat in hand, comes from his room.

Well, darling Torvald, did you get rid of him?

HELMER: Yes. He's gone.

NORA: Ah…meet Kristine who has come to town.

HELMER: Kristine? I beg your pardon I don't know…

NORA: Mrs Linde. Mrs Kristine Linde / dear Torvald.

HELMER: Yes. A childhood friend of my wife's…?

LINDE: Yes, we've known each / other a long time.

NORA: And imagine, she has travelled all this way
    Just to speak to you…

HELMER: What does that / mean, Nora…

LINDE: Not exactly / just…

NORA: Kristine is tremendously good at office
    Work and really wants to work under
    a very clever man /
    who will teach her so much more…

HELMER: Very sensible, / madam.

NORA: So when she heard that you had
    become director of a bank – by telegram!
    She hotfooted it to town and
    Isn't it a fact, Torvald…that you can
    Do something for her…just for me? /
    Darling. Please.

HELMER: Not impossible.
    You're a widow, presumably, madam?

LINDE: Yes.

HELMER: Experienced in office work?

LINDE: Very. Yes.

HELMER: Well, it's highly likely I can / offer you
something…

NORA claps her hands.

NORA: You see! You see!

HELMER: Lucky timing, Madam.

LINDE: How can I / thank you?

HELMER: Absolutely unnecessary puts on overcoat…
But now you must excuse me…

RANK: Wait, I'll come with you.

Collects fur coat, warms it by the stove.

NORA: Torvald don't be long.

HELMER: About an hour. / No longer.

NORA: Kristine, are you leaving as well?

LINDE: (*Outdoor clothes.*) …Yes…now I have to look /
For a room…

HELMER: Then we can go down / the road together…

NORA helps her.

How boring of us to live in such a small
Apartment! / …we just couldn't.

LINDE: Oh what are you thinking? Dear Nora
Goodbye. / And Thank you for everything.

NORA: Goodbye. For Now! You'll come back this
Evening of course. Yes! You too, Doctor Rank.
What? If you're well enough? Of course
You will be! Just wrap up well!

*During this conversation they enter the hall and the children's
voices are heard outside the door.*

Here they are! Here they are!

She runs to open the door. Nanny ANNE-MARIE with the children.

NORA: Come in, come in.

Bends down and kisses them.

…Oh
You sweeties! Look at them, Kristine / …Aren't they Heaven?

RANK: No talking in the cold. Illegal!

HELMER: Come on Mrs Linde.
Only mothers could bear this level of
Sweetness!

RANK, HELMER and LINDE go down the stairs.

ANNE-MARIE enters the room with children.

NORA does too and closes the hall door.

NORA: Here's a picture of Health.
What red cheeks you've got.
Apples and roses! Have you had lots of fun?
Well, that was just super!
Oh well…you pulled Emmy and Bob on the sled?
Two of Them? At The Same Time?
Yes, you are a clever boy, Ivar.
Let me hold her a minute, Anne Marie!
My sweet little doll-baby.
Yes, alright, Mummy will dance
With Bob too! What? You've been
throwing snowballs???
Oh I wish I'd joined in! No, not that…Anne Marie…
I want to undress them, Anne Marie. Oh yes, let me!
Yes…it is more fun… Go in…you look
Like a block of ice. There's hot coffee. Stove.

ANNE MARIE enters room SL.

NORA undresses children, throws coats anywhere while they all chatter.

A big bad dog chased you? Did it bite?
Dogs aren't allowed to bite lovely little
Doll children. No feeling the parcels Ivan!
What's in them? Horrible Things! So.
Shall we play? Hiding Games!???! Yes…let's
Play Hiding Games! Bob hide first. Shall I?
Yes, let me hide first!

The four play laughing and cheering, in the lounge and adjoining room R.

NORA hides under the table children come charging in looking. Stumped. Hear her muffled guffawing. Lift the cloth, see her. Storming cheers. She crawls out to scare them. More cheering.

Meanwhile, a knock at the door. Unheard KROGSTAD comes into view, he waits.

Game continues.

KROGSTAD: Excuse me! I beg your / pardon Mrs Helmer…

NORA: (*Jumps.*) Oh! What do you want?

KROGSTAD: Excuse me…the front door was open Someone must have forgotten / to close it…

NORA gets up.

NORA: My husband isn't here, / Mr Krogstad.

KROGSTAD: I know.

NORA: Yes. So what do you / want here then.

KROGSTAD: To speak to you.

NORA: With. (*To children.*) Go into Anne Marie.
What? No, the strange man won't hurt mummy.
When he's gone, we'll play again.

*She leads the children into the room L and closes the door
after them.*

You want to speak / to me?

KROGSTAD: Yes. I do.

NORA: Today? It's not the first of the / month.

KROGSTAD: No. It's Christmas Eve.
It's up to you if it's a Happy Christmas.

NORA: What do you want? Today I don't have / a mo…

KROGSTAD: This is something else.
And you do have a moment.

NORA: Yes. Well. I suppose I do.

KROGSTAD: Good. I was sitting in Olsen's café
And I saw your husband walk down the street.

NORA: Yes.

KROGSTAD: With a lady.

NORA: So?

KROGSTAD: May I ask if the lady was Mrs Linde?

NORA: Yes.

KROGSTAD: Just come to town.

NORA: Yes, today.

KROGSTAD: She is a good friend / of yours…

NORA: Yes. Why?

KROGSTAD: I knew her once too.

NORA: I know.

KROGSTAD: Oh…you know about that? I thought so.
Yes. Then I'll ask you straight out…
Is Mrs Linde going to get a post at
The / Joint Stock Bank?

NORA: How dare you question me, Mr Krogstad?
You are a subordinate of my husband's.
But since you dare…I'll answer.
Yes. She is. And I secured it for her.
Now you know.

KROGSTAD: I added it up right.

NORA: (*Walks up and down.*) …One does have a little
Influence. Even if one is a woman.
If One is in a subordinate position, one
Should really take care not to offend
Someone who / …

KROGSTAD: Wields that influence?

NORA: Exactly.

KROGSTAD: Mrs Helmer would you be so kind as to
wield.
That influence for my benefit?

NORA: What do you mean?

KROGSTAD: Would you be so kind as to ensure my
Subordinate position at the bank?

NORA: What are you talking about?
Who's thinking about endangering it?

KROGSTAD: Don't pretend to be stupid with Me.
I can imagine why your friend finds it
Unpleasant to keep running into me
And now I don't need to imagine who I
Can thank for / having me chased off

NORA: But I assure you…

KROGSTAD: Yes alright plain and simple.
There's still time
So I strongly advise you to use
Your influence and stop this

NORA: Mr Krogstad…I have no influence.

KROGSTAD: Now you have no influence…
I thought / you just said.

NORA: I didn't mean it like that. How can you
Think I have influence like that over my husband?

KROGSTAD: I know your husband. We were students
together.
I don't think Mr Bank Director
is any more firm than other husbands

NORA: If you insult my husband I'll show you the door.

KROGSTAD: Madam is brave.

NORA: I'm not afraid of you any more.
After New Year, I'll be rid of the whole business.

KROGSTAD grows more controlled.

KROGSTAD: Listen to me, Madam. If it is necessary
I will fight tooth and claw to keep my
Little job at the bank.

NORA: Clearly.

KROGSTAD: My salary is the least of it.
There's something else   now   yes out with it!
It is this.
You know   everybody does   that some
Years ago I made a bad mistake

NORA: I think I heard that yes.

KROGSTAD: It never came to court
   But after that all doors magically closed for me
   So I took up the business you know I do
   I had to live
   And I am not the worst
   But now I have to get out of it
   My sons are growing up
   For them I need to recover my
   Respectability and self regard
   This post was the very first rung on that ladder
   And your husband is going to kick away the ladder
   And I'll be standing in the dirt again.

NORA: Honestly Mr Krogstad
   It's not in my power to help you.

KROGSTAD: You don't have the inclination
   But I have the power to force you.

NORA: You wouldn't tell my husband I owe you money?

KROGSTAD: Wouldn't I?

NORA: Shame on you if you do!

   Almost crying.

   This secret is my pride and joy. I couldn't
   Bear he heard it in such an unpleasant vulgar!
   Way! And from you! How frightfully
   Unpleasant!

KROGSTAD: Just unpleasant?

NORA: (*Vehemently.*) Go on then, Do It. Let my
   Husband see you for what you are. See if
   You keep your little job then!

KROGSTAD: To repeat. Are you only afraid of
   Unpleasantness at home?

NORA: If my husband finds out…he'll pay you
   Immediately and then / we'll be shot of you.

KROGSTAD: (*A pace nearer.*) …Listen Mrs Helmer…is your
Memory going?…or do you really have
So little business sense?
I see I'll have to educate you a little.

NORA: How?

KROGSTAD: When your husband was ill…
You came to me to borrow / four thousand eight hundred
crowns…

NORA: I didn't know anyone / else.

KROGSTAD: And I promised to get you that / amount…

NORA: And you did / get it.

KROGSTAD: I promised you that amount on certain
Conditions. You were so concerned
About your husband's health, so desperate to
Travel that I don't think you paid much attention
to the terms of our contract.
Let me therefore remind me. I promised
To get the money against a promissory note…
which I drew / up…

NORA: Yes. Which I signed.

KROGSTAD: Good. But then I added in a clause
Which was for your father to
guarantee the debt. Which he was to sign.

NORA: Was to…? He did sign.

KROGSTAD: I left the date blank…
That is…your father was to fill in the date
On the day he signed the clause.
Does madam remember that?

NORA: Yes…I think so…

KROGSTAD: I then handed you the note to post to your
Father. Yes?

NORA: Yes

KROGSTAD: Which you must have done immediately…
    Because five, six days later you brought me
    The note with your father's signature.
    And you got your money.

NORA: Yes. Well, haven't I kept up the payments?

KROGSTAD: More or less… But…to return to this time…
    It was a very hard time for you, was it?

NORA: Yes it was.

KROGSTAD: Your father was very ill, wasn't he?

NORA: He was dying.

KROGSTAD: And indeed, died shortly afterwards.

NORA: Yes.

KROGSTAD: Mrs Helmer…do you remember the
    Day he died? The exact day and month, I mean…

NORA: Pappa died on the 29th of September.

KROGSTAD: That's right. I checked. Which leaves
    Us with an something odd…

    Takes out paper.

    Which I simply / can't explain…

NORA: Something Odd? / I don't know…

KROGSTAD: Very odd… Your father signed this note
    Three days after his death.

NORA: How? I don't understand.

KROGSTAD: Your father died on the 29th September.
    But look here.
    Your father dated his signature October 2nd.
    Isn't that odd Madam?

NORA is silent

Can you explain that?

NORA says nothing.

What is also odd is…
The 2nd October…and the year, look!…
Are not in your father's hand…
But in a hand I seem to recognise.
Well…it can all make sense.
Your father could have forgotten to
Date his signature…and someone
Else might have just guessed it
Before they knew when he died!
Nothing wrong with that.
It's the signature that matters.
I assume that it is genuine Mrs Helmer?
It really was your Pappa himself
Who has written his name here?

After a brief silence NORA throws back her head and looks at him defiantly.

NORA: No it wasn't. I signed Pappa's name.

KROGSTAD: Madam you know how dangerous this
　　Confession is?

NORA: Why? You'll soon get your / money.

KROGSTAD: Can I ask you something?
　　Why didn't you send the paper to
　　Your father?

NORA: It was impossible.
　　Pappa was lying there ill!
　　If I'd asked for him to sign
　　I'd have had to tell him what it was for!
　　How could I tell my ill father how
　　My husband's life was in such danger?
　　It was impossible!

KROGSTAD: Then you should have given up on the
    Journey abroad!

NORA: That was impossible too! A trip to
    Save my husband's life! How could I?

KROGSTAD: Didn't it occur to you this was a fraud
    Against me?

NORA: I couldn't think about that. I didn't care
    About you. I couldn't bear you, putting
    Your icy conditions in my path when
    You knew the danger my husband was in!

KROGSTAD: Mrs Helmer, I don't think you have a clue
    what
    You are guilty of. Let me enlighten you.
    It is nothing more and nothing worse
    Than that one thing I once did
    Which destroyed my reputation.

NORA: You? You're asking *me* to believe
    That *you* did something brave
    to save your wife's life?

KROGSTAD: The law isn't interested in motive.

NORA: Then the law is bad!

KROGSTAD: Bad or not…I present this paper in court
    You'll be judged by that law.

NORA: I don't believe you. A daughter can't protect
    Her old dying father?
    A wife can't save her husband's life?
    I don't know the law very well, but I'm
    Sure somewhere it says this is justifiable!
    And if you don't know that, you Mr Krogstad, must
    Be a very bad lawyer!

KROGSTAD: Maybe I am…
    But don't you think I'm a good judge of our

Mutual business here?
Yes? Good.
Do what you like…
But I warn you…
If I am thrown out into the cold a second time
You will keep me company there

He exits through the hall.

NORA thinks for a time. Then tosses her head.

NORA: He's just trying to frighten me.
Well, that's not as easy as he thinks!

She sets to collecting the children's scattered things. Stops.

But?
No but that is impossible.
I did it out of love, didn't I?

The children are in the doorway SL.

CHILDREN: Mamma, the strange man just went out
Through the gate!

NORA: Yes I know
But don't tell anyone about the strange man.
Are you listening? Not even Pappa.

CHILDREN: No mamma. Will you play with us now?

NORA: Not now. No.

CHILDREN: Mamma, you promised!

NORA: Yes. But I can't now. I've so much to do.
Go in, go in.
You're my dearest sweetest children.

*She chivvies them gently into the room and closes the door
behind them She sits on the sofa and takes up her embroidery.
A couple of stitches, then stops.*

No.

She throws the embroidery aside, gets up, shouts from the hall door.

Helene!
Let me have the tree in here.

Goes to the table, SL, opens the drawer, but stops again.

No. This is impossible.

HELENE enters with the Christmas tree.

HELENE: Where shall I put it, Madam?

NORA: There. The middle of the floor.

HELENE: Shall I bring anything else?

NORA: No thank you. I have what I need.

HELENE exits and NORA starts to decorate the tree.

Candles here   flowers here
That loathsome man!
Talk talk talk!
There's nothing the matter.
The Christmas tree is going to be
Lovely.
I will do all that Torvald wishes
Sing
Dance.

HELMER enters from the hall with a bundle of papers under his arm.

Oh, you're back!

HELMER: Yes. Did anyone call?

NORA: Here? No.

HELMER: Odd. I saw Krogstad go out the front gate.

NORA: Oh? Oh yes, that's true.

KROGSTAD was here for a moment.

HELMER: Nora, I can read you like a very slim book.
   He was here and asked you to put a good word
   In for him.

NORA: Yes.

HELMER: And you were to pretend it was your idea.
   And you were to pretend he wasn't here.
   Yes?

NORA: Yes / but…

HELMER: Nora Nora, how do you get into these things?
   You talk to such a man you promise him
   Something
   And then you tell me a lie…

NORA: A lie?

HELMER: Didn't you say no-one had been here?

Wags his finger.

The More Hen mustn't do that Ever More.
The bird must sing a pure song.
No lies in its crop.

Holds her round the waist

That's how it should be. Yes?

He lets her go.

So no more about it.

He sits down in front of the stove.

It's so warm and cosy in here.

He leafs through the papers.

NORA busies herself with the tree.

A short pause.

NORA: Torvald.

HELMER: Yes?

NORA: I'm so tremendously looking forward
    To the Stenborgs Fancy Dress Party! /
    The day after tomorrow!!!

HELMER: And I'm tremendously looking forward to see
    What you'll surprise me with.

NORA: Oh, it's a terrible idea!

HELMER: What is?

NORA: I can't come up with anything.
    Everything seems so silly so meaningless.

HELMER: Has little Nora decided that?

NORA is behind his chair, resting her arms on the back.

NORA: Torvald, are you terribly busy?

HELMER: Well.

NORA: What are those papers?

HELMER: Bank business.

NORA: Already?

HELMER: I've got the board to give me
    Full authority to implement policy and
    Staff changes. I've to do it over Christmas.
    By New Year I want everything in order.

NORA: So that's why this poor man / Krogstad…

HELMER: Hmmm.

NORA: (*Still over the chair back, slowly messing up his hair.*)
    If you weren't so terribly busy…
    I would ask you a really really big favour, Torvald…

HELMER: Let's hear it. Make your case.

NORA: Well…no-one has better taste than you.
    I want to look so good at the party.
    Torvald, will you decide what I should go as
    And what I should wear?

HELMER: Is prosecution now wanting special pleading?

NORA: She is. She needs your special help.

HELMER: Good. I'll consider the case.
    We'll come to a decision.

NORA: Oh how kind you are. M'Lud.

    Walks back to the tree. Pause.

    These red flowers are so handsome.
    But tell me…is what this Krogstad did…
    Really so bad?

HELMER: Forging signatures? Have you any idea
    What that means?

NORA: Perhaps he did it out of necessity…

HELMER: Yes…or, like so many, out of imprudence!
    I'm not so heartless
    That I'd condemn a man outright for one
    Mistake.

NORA: Wouldn't you, Torvald?

HELMER: No. Many a man can come about morally
    If he admits to his guilt
    And takes his punishment.

NORA: Punishment?

HELMER: But he didn't chose that path.
    He carries on using tricks and
    Deceit ! And that is what has made him
    A moral disgrace!

NORA: Do you think / it should…

HELMER: Imagine how someone so guilty has to
    Lie and cheat and pretend to everyone…
    wear a mask in front of his nearest and dearest…
    yes, even with his wife his children…
    With his children!
    That, Nora, is the most dreadful part of it!

NORA: Why?

HELMER: because such a reeking circle of lies brings…
    infection…and virtually…disease…into the life
    of the entire home
    So every breath the children take
    In such a home is teeming with the germs of
    something bad ugly.

NORA: (*Behind him.*) Is that what you think?

HELMER: Oh my dear, I've seen it enough as a lawyer.
    Nearly every young offender has had
    A Lying mendacious mother…

NORA: Why just…mothers?

HELMER: It can most frequently be traced back to the
    mothers. But fathers contribute of course.
    Any lawyer knows that.
    This Krogstad has gone home year in year out
    Infecting his own children's minds
    With his lies and deceit.
    That's why I'd term him 'morally lost.'

He stretches out his hands towards her.

Ergo, my sweet little Nora must swear not
To plead his case.

Your hand on it.
Now now what's this?
Give me your hand.
See then. Decided then.
I assure you, it would have been
Hopeless for me to work with him.
I literally feel sick to my soul
In the presence of such people…

NORA withdraws her hand and goes to the other side of the Christmas tree.

NORA: How hot it is in here.
And I have so much to do.

HELMER gets up and gathers his papers.

HELMER: Yes, I should think about reading some
Of this before dinner. And I need to
Think about your costume. And I
Might have something to wrap in gold paper
And hang on this tree.

He puts his hand on her head.

Bless you…my Christmas robin.

He enters the study, closes the door behind him.

NORA, after a pause, quietly.

NORA: Oh what? It is not so. It is impossible.
It must be impossible.

ANNE MARIE appears in the doorway, SL.

ANNE MARIE: The little ones ask very sweetly
Can they come to Mamma?

NORA: No, no, no, don't let them in to me!
You stay with them Anne-Marie.

ANNE MARIE: Yes. Yes, madam.

ANNE MARIE closes the door.

NORA pale from fear.

NORA: Corrupt my children?
Poison my home?

Short pause. She raises her head.

That will never be true. Not in all eternity.

End of Act One.

ACT TWO

Christmas Day

The same room. In the corner by the piano stands the Christmas tree, picked clean, its candles burned down.

NORA, alone, walks about uneasily. She stops by the sofa. Takes up her coat.

NORA: (*Drops her coat.*) Someone's coming! (*Listens at the door.*) Nobody. Of course not.
It's Christmas Day! Nobody will come today! Or Tomorrow. But… (*Opens the door. Looks out.*)
No. Nothing in the letter box. Empty. (*Walks across the floor.*) Stop this foolishness! He wont Do Anything About It. These Things Don't Happen. It's impossible. I have three children!

ANNE MARIE enters from the room L with a large cardboard box.

ANNE MARIE: So. I've found the dressing up box.

NORA: Thank you. Put it on the table.

ANNE MARIE does so.

ANNE MARIE: They're in a terrible mess.

NORA: I wish I could tear it all into a Hundred thousand pieces!

ANNE MARIE: Preserve us! They can be sorted out. Just a little patience.

NORA: Yes I'll get Mrs Linde to help me.

ANNE MARIE: Out again? In this weather? You'll catch Your death!

NORA: There's worse things. How are the children?

ANNE MARIE: The poor scraps are playing with their
    presents / …
    But…

NORA: Are they still asking for me?

ANNE MARIE: Well, they're so used to having Mamma
    around…

NORA: Yes, well, Anne Marie, from now on I can't
    Be with them as much.

ANNE MARIE: Now…small children get used to all sorts
    of
    Things.

NORA: Do you think so? Do you think they'd forget
    Their mother if she was completely gone?

ANNE MARIE: Preserve us! Completely gone!

NORA: Listen tell me Anne Marie…
    I keep thinking about it
    …how could your heart bear to give
    Your child to a stranger?

ANNE MARIE: Well, I had to, didn't I? I had to be wet
    nurse
    To baby Nora.

NORA: Yes but was that what you wanted?

ANNE MARIE: When I could get such a good position?
    A poor unfortunate girl, I was so lucky.
    That man wasn't prepared
    To do anything about it!

NORA: But your daughter must have forgotten all
    About you.

ANNE MARIE: Indeed she hasn't. She's written twice!
After her confirmation and when she
Got married!

NORA touches her neck.

NORA: You old Anne-Marie   you were a good mother
To me when I was little.

ANNE MARIE: You Little Nora. The poor thing had no other
Mother but me.

NORA: And if the littlies had no mother...I know
That you would...talktalktalk.

She opens the box.

Go to them. Now I must...tomorrow you'll
See / how lovely I can be.

ANNE MARIE: There'll be no-one at the ball as lovely as
Little Nora.

ANNE MARIE goes into the room L.

NORA begins to unpack the box but casts it all aside...

NORA: Oh if I dared go out! If only no one came!
If only nothing happened in the meantime here!
Stupid talk. No-one is coming. Just. Don't. Think.
Brush off the muff. Lovely gloves. Lovely gloves.
Get rid of it. Get rid of it.
One two three four five six...
(*Cries out.*) Oh, they are coming!

She wants to go to the door but can't.

MRS LINDE enters from the hall where she's left her outdoor clothes.

Oh, is it you, Kristine? No-one else?
How good it's You.

LINDE: I heard you'd come by asking for me.

NORA: Yes. I was just passing.
  There is something you
  Absolutely must help me with. Sit on the sofa.
  Look. There's a Fancy Dress Party tomorrow night
  Upstairs at Consul Stenborg's!
  and Torvald wants me to be
  'A Neapolitan fisher girl'!
  And 'Dance the Tarantella'!
  (*Grand.*) For I learned it on Capri…

LINDE: Really? You're giving A Full Performance?

NORA: Torvald says I should. See, I have the costume.
  Torvald had it made for me…but now its
  Falling to bits and / I just don't know…

LINDE: We can mend it. Its just the fringes that
  Have come loose…Needle and thread?
  Now, we have what we need.

NORA: You're so kind.

  LINDE sews.

  So you'll be all in disguise, tomorrow, Nora?
  Do you know…I think I'll pop round and
  See you all dressed up… Masked!
  …I forgot to thank
  You for such a charming evening yesterday.

NORA: Oh I don't think it was as charming as usual!
  You should have hit town a bit sooner, Kristine
  Yes, Torvald certainly knows how to make
  A home charming.

LINDE: So do you. You're not your father's daughter
  For nothing.
  Is Dr Rank usually so depressed?

NORA: No. Yesterday it was very noticeable.
    He has a very serious illness. He suffers from
    Wasting of the spinal cord, poor man.
    His father was repulsive. He kept mistresses
    And such. That is why the poor little son
    Became sickly…if you follow me.

LINDE lets the sewing drop.

LINDE: But dearest, bestest Nora, how do you
    Know these things?

NORA: (*Walks about.*) Puh…when one has three
    Children one gets visits from…from women
    Who know a thing or two…and tell one
    a thing or two…

LINDE sews again. Short silence.

    Does Doctor Rank
    Drop by every day?

NORA: Every single day. He's Torvald's oldest Bestest
    Friend and my good friend too. Doctor
    Rank kind of belongs in this house.

LINDE: Is he a sincere man? I mean…
    Does he like to flatter?

NORA: No, on the contrary.
    Why do you say that?

LINDE: When you introduced me to him…
    He said he often heard me talked about here.
    But then I noticed…your husband had
    No idea who I actually was. /
    How could Doctor Rank…

NORA: Oh yes, that's right Kristine
    Well, Torvald is so indescribably fond of me
    He wants me all to himself. When we were

First married he became quite jealous if I
Mentioned my loved ones from home. So naturally
I stopped. But with Doctor Rank
I speak about these things...because he he
Likes to hear about them / you see.

LINDE: Listen Nora. You're still The Child. I'm
Still The Grownup-One With Experience.
I want to say something. You should
Stop all this with Doctor Rank.

NORA: Stop all what?

LINDE: All this! The rich admirer! Who
Can leave you all his money.

NORA: Who doesn't exist. Unfortunately! /
What are you...

LINDE: Is Doctor Rank rich?

NORA: Ooh yes.

LINDE: And no-one to provide for?

NORA: No one / but...

LINDE: And he comes to this house every day?

NORA: I've said / so, yes.

LINDE: How can this delicate man be so indelicate?

NORA: I don't understand a word you're saying.

LINDE: Nora, stop pretending. Don't you think
I haven't guessed who lent you the four thousand eight
hundred crowns?

NORA laughs.

NORA: You've gone mad! Your imagination!
A friend! Who comes here *every day*?
Wouldn't that be frightfully embarrassing?

LINDE: So it's not him?

NORA: Of course not! It never occurred to me...
Ah...! He had nothing then! He inherited / it later!

LINDE: Just as well, Nora.

NORA: It would never enter my head to ask Doctor Rank...
Mind you ...I'm sure If I / were to ...

LINDE: But you won't.

NORA: Of course not! I don't think it will be necessary...
But I'm sure if I mentioned it to Doctor Rank...

LINDE: Behind your husband's back?

NORA: But I have to get out of this other thing...
Which is also behind / his back...

LINDE: Yes yes I said that yesterday but...

NORA: (*Pacing.*) A man can manage these things
much better / than a woman...

LINDE: Her own husband, yes.

NORA: Nonsense. (*Stops.*) When you pay all you owe...
your contract's over / isn't it?

LINDE: Yes. / Obviously.

NORA: And you can tear it up into a hundred thousand
Pieces and burn it up...
the horrid disgusting bit of paper?

LINDE puts down the sewing gets up and confronts NORA.

LINDE: Nora You're hiding something from me.

NORA: Can you tell?

LINDE: Something's happened since yesterday.
What is / it Nora?

NORA: Kristine listens. Ssh. Torvald's home.
Go in and sit with the children. Torvald can't bear to
See 'sewing'. Let Anne-Marie help you.

LINDE gathers up the sewing.

LINDE: All right…but I'm not leaving until
We have really spoken.

She exits SL, at the same time, HELMER enters from the hall.

NORA goes to him.

NORA: Oh, I've been waiting for you, Torvald!

HELMER: Was that the dressmaker?

NORA: No. Kristine. She's helping me mend my costume.
I'm going to look lovely.

HELMER: Of course you are. Wasn't it a good idea I had?

NORA: Splendid. But aren't I good to go along with it?

HELMER: (*Takes her under her chin.*) Good – to (*Mock severe.*)
go along with your husband?
Don't attack me…I know
That's not what you mean. I wont disturb you.
You need to rehearse, don't you?

NORA: And you need to work.

HELMER: Yes. (*Shows her a bundle of man-type papers.*) See
I've been to the bank… (*Goes to his room.*)

NORA: Torvald.

HELMER: Yes.

NORA: Say your squirrel asked from her heart
Beautifully for you to do / something.

HELMER: What?

NORA: Would you do / it?

HELMER: I would have to know what / it is first.

NORA: The squirrel would run up and down on you
    And do tricks if you're kind and does /
    What she asks.

HELMER: Out with it then.

NORA: The lark would skylark in all the rooms /
    Up and down.

HELMER: Which she does / anyway.

NORA: She would play elf-girl and dance for you in
    The moonlight, / Torvald.

HELMER: Nora, it isn't what we talked
    about this morning is it?

NORA moves closer.

NORA: Yes Torvald.
    I beg you from the bottom of my heart.

HELMER: You really have the heart to rip open / this case
    again?

NORA: Yes You must indulge me. You must let
    Krogstad keep his position / at the bank.

HELMER: My dear Nora, I've decided to give his job to
    Mrs Linde.

NORA: That is tremendously kind of you.
    But you can just fire someone else / instead
    Of Krogstad.

HELMER: I can't believe how stubborn you are.
    Just because you've made him a foolish
    Promise, / I have to.

NORA: That's not why, Torvald. It's for your sake.
This man writes in the most awful newspapers
You said so yourself. He can harm you.
I'm haunted by him.

HELMER: Aha. I understand. Haunting you.
It is old memories.

NORA: What do you mean by that?

HELMER: You're thinking about your father.

NORA: Yes. Yes. Remember the malicious things people
Wrote and whispered behind his back.
Terrible. Horrible,
I'm sure he would have been dismissed
if they hadn't sent you to investigate…
and if you hadn't been so kind / and helpful to him…

HELMER: My little Nora, there's a world of difference
between me and your father.
Your father was not irreproachable.
But I am. And hope to be so, as long as I hold
This position…

NORA: But no-one knows what bad people might make up.
We could be so comfortable so quiet, so calm in
Our peaceful carefree home…you and I and the
Children Torvald!
/ That's why I really really ask from my heart.

HELMER: The more you plead, the more impossible it is
To keep him. The bank already knows I'm
Dismissing him. If it got out that the new /
Bank manager let's his wife change his mind.

NORA: So what then?

HELMER: So, for Miss Always-Gets-Her-Way
…I become a laughing stock with my whole staff.
People will think I've no mind of my own.

Anyway…there's another reason why
Krogstad / can't be…

NORA: What?

HELMER: At a pinch I could have overlooked / his moral
failings…

NORA: You could Torvald.

HELMER: And he's supposed to be quite good…
But he's a boyhood friend. One of those
Stupid relationships that come back to kick you
In the face! We know each other. And he's too
Insensitive to hide it in front of people who count!
No…he adopts this familiar tone with me…comes
The 'Helmer! Old Boy! 'The Embarrassment!
My position would be intolerable!

NORA: Torvald, you don't mean this.

HELMER: Don't mean what?

NORA: This petty-mindedness.

HELMER: Pettymindedness? Are you saying I'm /
petty minded?

NORA: Absolutely not! It's because you're / not.

HELMER: Alright. If you say my actions my petty minded
Then that makes me petty minded, doesn't it?
Absolutely! Alright, let's be done with it…

Goes to the hall. Calls.

Helene!

NORA: Oh, what are you doing?

HELMER, taking a decision, searches through his papers.

HELENE comes in.

See… Take this letter. Straight away.
Get hold of a delivery man. Quickly.
Address is on the outside. Look…here's the
Money…

HELENE: Very good, Sir.

She goes with the letter.

HELMER puts his papers together.

HELMER: There now, Miss Long Face.

NORA: (*Breathless.*) Torvald what was that letter?

HELMER: Krogstad's dismissal letter.

NORA: Get it back! Torvald! There's time! Torvald!
Get it back! For my sake! For your own for the
Children's sake! Are you listening??? Torvald
Do It! You have no idea what this means for Us!

HELMER: Too late.

NORA: Yes. Too late.

HELMER: Dear Nora I'm going to forgive this slur
On my character oh yes it is! Me afraid of
A tired-out starving scurrilous Hack Writer?
I'm going to forgive you because Darling
It shows how much you love me.

He takes her in his arms.

It's gone. Que sera sera. Whatever will be will be…
I've got both the courage and the power for
Anything. You'll see what kind of man I am.
I'll take everything upon myself!

NORA: (*Terror-stricken.*) What do you mean by that?

HELMER: Everything / I say.

NORA: You won't. Not in all eternity.

HELMER: Good. We'll both take it on. Man and wife.
Like it should be. Satisfied? No, not those
Petrified Pigeon Eyes! It's all just 'Fevered
Imaginings!!'
Now tarantella rehearsal tambourine practice!
I'll retire to the inner office and close the door
Thus hearing Nothing!
Make all the noise you want.
When Rank arrives tell him where I am.

He nods to her, goes with his papers into his room and closes the door behind him.

NORA, wild with anxiety and dread stands as if nailed fast.

NORA: (*Whispers.*) He's capable of doing it
He'll do it. He will do it.
Despite everything in the whole world!
No, not in all eternity!
Before everything else!
Rescue! A way out...

Bell rings in the hall.

Doctor Rank!
Before everything else...whatever it shall be!

She wipes her face with her hand, pulls herself together, goes and opens the door to the hall.

DR RANK stands hanging up his fur overcoat. During the following, it begins to get dark...

NORA: Merry Christmas, Doctor Rank.
I recognised your elfin ring.
But you shall not go in to Torvald now
I don't think he's got a moment to spare

RANK: And you?

As he comes into the room and she closes the door behind him.

NORA: Oh, you know me…I've always got a moment
  To spare for you…

RANK: I'm glad. I'll borrow those moments as long as
  I can.

NORA: What do you mean?

RANK: I mean as long as I can. Does that scare you?

NORA: Yes.
  Is something going to happen?

RANK: Only what I've been prepared for for ages.
  I just didn't think it would be so soon.

  NORA grasps his arm.

NORA: What have you found out?
  Doctor Rank, you must tell me!

RANK: The line on my chart is going down
  and down sits by stove
  Nothing to do about it.

NORA: (*Breathes relieved.*) Your diagnosis?

RANK: My diagnosis. Pointless lying to oneself.
  My most pathetic patient? Me!
  I've just run a full feasibility check
  On this business here. Bankruptcy.
  Spent. Within a month I'll be in
  Liquidation in the churchyard.

NORA: Oh shh… Horrid ugly words…

RANK: Horrid ugly Thing. The horridest ugliest
  Thing being the horrid ugliness up ahead
  Got the one more examination to put
  Myself through learn exactly
  When the liquidation will begin.
  There's something I want to say to you
  Helmer can't stand this sort of sickroom

Nonsense. Never had the stomach for it…
So…I won't have him in my sick room…

NORA: Oh but / Doctor Rank.

RANK: No absolutely not. Forbidden. Illegal!
As soon as I've heard the worst…
I'll send you my visiting card…
With a black cross on it
And then you know
Destruction's Abomination Has Begun…

NORA: No. You're So unreasonable today.
And I so very much wanted you in A Good Mood!

RANK: While carrying Death in my hands?
The Death Penalty for someone else's Crime?
Where's the Justice in That?
That's Family Law for you!

NORA: (*Covers her ears.*) Ghoulish Nonsense!
Happy! Jolly! Merry!

RANK: Yes…and my soul the joke!
The laugh's on my poor innocent spine
For Daddy's Jolly Soldiering!

NORA: (*By the table.*) He was addicted to asparagus.
And goose-liver pate. Wasn't he?

RANK: Oh yes. And truffles.

NORA: Truffles, yes. And oysters I believe?

RANK: Oysters yes. Oysters. Naturally.

NORA: And then all the port
And champagne.
It's God's joke to make such delicious
Things so dangerous.

RANK: And let them attack a pile of bones
Who never got the least bit of pleasure from them.

NORA: Well that is the most tragic thing of all.

RANK: (*Looking searchingly at her.*) Hmmm?

NORA: (*A little after.*) Why did you smile?

RANK: No it was you who laughed.

NORA: I put it to you it was you who smiled Doctor Rank!

RANK: No, I put it to you. (*Gets up.*) You are a greater rogue
    Than even I imagined.

NORA: I am bent on roguery today.

RANK: So it would seem.

NORA: (*Both hands on his shoulders.*)
    Dear, dear Doctor Rank, you are not allowed to
    Leave Torvald and me.

RANK: You'll recover. Doctor's diagnosis.
    The one who goes is soon forgotten.

NORA: (*Anxious.*) Do you think so?

RANK: New friends arrive. / And then…

NORA: What new friends? Who does?

RANK: Helmer. You. Already you…this
    Mrs Linde / yesterday evening…

NORA: Aha…you're jealous of Kristine!

RANK: Yes I am! She's my successor.
    When I can't come into this house
    This female…

NORA: Shhh…quiet…she is in there.

RANK: Already! You see!

NORA: To sew my costume! You're so
    Unreasonable! Be kind, Doctor Rank.

Tomorrow you'll get to see how
Beautifully I dance…and imagine I
Dance just for you…and just for Torvald
Of course obviously…

She's taking different things from the box…

Doctor Rank sit down here
I want to show you something…

RANK: (*Sits.*) What?

NORA: This!

RANK: Silk stockings.

NORA: Flesh-coloured! Aren't they lovely?
It's so dark now…but tomorrow…
No no no you only get to see the feet!
Well…perhaps a little higher…

RANK: Hmm…

NORA: Oh why so critical?
Do you think they're unsuitable?

RANK: A simple doctor – beyond my medical knowledge.

NORA: (*Looks at him a moment.*) Shame on you! (*Hits him
lightly on the ear with the stockings.*) Take that!

RANK: What other delights do you want me to examine?

NORA: Not one more thing. You are a very bad doctor.

RANK: (*After a short silence.*) When I'm sitting here
With you like this I cannot think no
What would have happened to me if I'd
Never come to this house.

NORA: (*Smiles.*) Well I do believe that when we
Get right down to it…you quite enjoy
Yourself here…

RANK: (*Quieter, looks at her.*) So to have to
Leave it all.

NORA: Shhh. You are not going to leave it all.

RANK: (*As before.*) And not be able to leave behind
One tiny token of thanks even other than
An empty seat which can be sat in / by
The first person...

NORA: If I asked you now about / ...No

RANK: About what?

NORA: About a large token of your / friendship...

RANK: Yes, Yes?

NORA: No I mean a tremendous / token of thanks...

RANK: Would you just once make me so happy?

NORA: Oh but you don't know what it is!

RANK: So say it!

NORA: No. I can't. It's so unreasonable...
All advice and help and / favour all...

RANK: The more the better! Whatever it is!
Tell me. In Confidence!

NORA: Which you have like no other! My most
Faithful and best friend! You know you are!
So...there is something you must help me
Prevent. You know how dearly how much
Torvald loves me...he wouldn't think twice
About sacrificing his life for me...

RANK: And you think he's the only one...?

NORA: What?

RANK: Who'd gladly sacrifice his life for you.

NORA: (*Heavily.*) Yes. So.

RANK: I've sworn to myself to let you know before
I died. There'll never be a better opportunity.
Yes Nora, now you know.
And you also know you can confide in me
As you can nobody else.

NORA gets up calmly.

Allow me to get by.

RANK: (*Makes space for her but remains sitting.*) Nora.

NORA: (*In the hallway.*) Helene bring the lamp. (*Goes over to
the stove.*) Ah dear Doctor Rank
That was really bad of you.

RANK: (*Gets up.*) That I have loved you as dearly as
Anybody? Ever? Was that bad?

NORA: No But to go and tell me so unnecessary.

RANK: What do you mean? Have you known then…

HELENE comes in with the lamp puts it on the table, exits.

RANK: Nora! Mrs Helmer have you known all…

NORA: Oh what do I know about what I have
And haven't known?
I really can't tell! That you could be so
Clumsy, Doctor Rank! When everything
Was so nice!

RANK: At least now you can be sure I am at your
Service life and soul. Finish what you were saying…

NORA: Even after… (*What just happened.*)

RANK: Especially after… Please.

NORA: You get nothing now.

RANK: Yes Yes! You mustn't punish me!
    Let me do something for you! If it
    Is within human capability!

NORA: Now you can do nothing for me.
    Besides I don't seem to need any help.
    You'll see that it was all in my imagination.
    Yes of course. Obviously.

Sits in the rocking chair, smiles

    Oh yes, you are indeed a fine fellow,
    Doctor Rank. Don't you think Shame On
    You now the lamp has been brought in?

RANK: No. Not really. But perhaps I should go
    …for good?

NORA: No you will not! You will come here just as
    Before. You know Torvald can't manage
    Without you.

RANK: Yes. But you?

NORA: Oh, I always think it is so terribly amusing
    When you come.

RANK: You see *that* is what confuses me!
    You are the *Sphinx* to me!
    Do you know how many times I've thought
    You might just as well have been with me
    As Torvald?

NORA: Yes. I do see.
    But do you see there are
    some people you care for most
    And others who you would almost rather be with…

RANK: Yes there's something in that

NORA: When I was at home I was most fond of Pappa.
    But it was the most tremendous fun to

Steal down into the maids room
Where I wasn't Guided!
And they just said any old thing!

RANK: It's the Maids I have replaced

NORA: (*Runs up and over to him.*) Oh dear kind Doctor
Rank I didn't mean it like that!
But you can understand how with
Torvald it is just like with Pappa…

HELENE enters from the hall.

HELENE: Madam!

She whispers and gives her a card.

NORA: (*Glances at the card.*) Ah! (*Puts it in her pocket.*)

RANK: Anything wrong?

NORA: No No! Just something my new costume

RANK: Your costume is lying there.

NORA: Oh yes. This is another   I ordered it
Torvald must know nothing.

RANK: Aha. Revealed! The Great Secret!

NORA: Absolutely! Go into him he's sitting
In there! Keep him occupied…

RANK: Be calm, be tranquil. He shall not
Escape my clutches.

Enters HELMER's room.

NORA: (*To HELENE.*) And he's standing waiting in
The kitchen?

HELENE: Yes he came up the back stairs

NORA: Didn't you say someone was here?

HELENE: Yes. Took no notice.

NORA: He won't leave????

HELENE: No, not till he's spoken to Madam.

NORA: Then let him in. But quietly, Helene...
    You mustn't say anything to anybody.
    It's a surprise for my husband!

HELENE: (*Yeah, right!*) Yes I understand. (*Goes out.*)

NORA: The Terrible Thing is happening.
    It is coming anyway!
    No no no it cannot happen.
    It cannot happen.

She bolts HELMER's door.

HELENE opens the hall door for KROGSTAD and shuts it behind him. He is dressed in travel furs, outdoor boots, fur hat.

NORA: Speak quietly, my husband is at home.

KROGSTAD: What if he is?

NORA: What do you want from me?

KROGSTAD: To let you know something.

NORA: What? Hurry up.

KROGSTAD: You know I've been dismissed?

NORA: I couldn't stop it Herr Krogstad
    I tried my absolute best
    But I couldn't help it.

KROGSTAD: Your husband loves you so little?
    He knows how I can expose you
    But yet he / dares to...

NORA: How do you think he got to / know about...

KROGSTAD: Oh I didn't think it. It isn't at all like
My chum Torvald Helmer to show
Such manly / courage…

NORA: Herr Krogstad, I demand respect / for my husband!

KROGSTAD: Respect? Of course! And since Madam is here
So carefully hiding her little secret, I can only assume
She has more idea today what she has actually done?

NORA: Yes. More than you could possibly know.

KROGSTAD: From such a poor lawyer as I…

NORA: What is it you want from me?

KROGSTAD: Just to see how you are, Mrs Helmer. You've been
On my mind all day. Even a debt collector…even
A man of the gutter press…can have a heart.

NORA: Then show it. Think of my children.

KROGSTAD: Have you and your husband thought about mine?
It doesn't matter. I just wanted to say…don't take
It too seriously… I'm not pursuing this matter
Further at this moment in time.

NORA: Oh, I knew you wouldn't…

KROGSTAD: We can sort it out amicably…just the three of us.

NORA: My husband must never find out.

KROGSTAD: How will you stop that? Perhaps you can pay
Me the outstanding balance?

NORA: No. Not immediately.

KROGSTAD: Or find some way of raising the money in the
Next / few days…?

NORA: No way I care to find.

KROGSTAD: And pointless anyway…if you stood here with
Fistfuls of crowns…I wouldn't part
With your note.

NORA: Tell me what you're going to do with it

KROGSTAD: I just want to keep it. Have it in My Care.
No-one it does not concern shall see it.
Just…if you were contemplating any desperate /
Measures…

NORA: I am.

KROGSTAD: Like…running away…

NORA: I am.

KROGSTAD: …or something even worse…

NORA: How did you know…?

KROGSTAD: forget about it.

NORA: How did you know I was thinking about that?

KROGSTAD: 'We' always think about it at first. I thought about it.
Too…I had the soul…but not the courage.

NORA: (*Tonelessly.*) Nor I.

KROGSTAD: (*Relieved.*) No you haven't the courage either, Have you?

NORA: No I haven't. I haven't.

KROGSTAD: It would be very stupid. Once the first
Domestic storm blows over…I have a letter to
Your husband in my pocket…

NORA: Telling everything?

KROGSTAD: As nicely as possible.

NORA: (*Fast.*) He mustn't read it. Tear it up.
I'll find a way of getting the money.

KROGSTAD: I'm sorry, I though I just explained / Madam.

NORA: I'm not talking about the money I owe you.
Tell me how much money you're demanding
From my husband…and I'll get it for you.

KROGSTAD: I'm not demanding money from / your
husband.

NORA: What are you demanding?

KROGSTAD: I'll tell you. I want a foothold, madam. On
The ladder back up
Your husband can help me onto that first rung.
I haven't told a lie for a year and a half!
And all that time…I was poor as a church mouse.
But I was happy that I was climbing
Step by step!
Now the ladder's been taken away.
Well, I'm not starting at the bottom again.
I'm climbing. I want to be back in the bank.
This time Higher. Your husband is going
To give / me a leg up…

NORA: No he is not!

KROGSTAD: Yes. He is! I know him. He daren't say a
thing!
And once I am in…watch me! Within a year, I'll
Be Mr Bank Director's right hand.

It'll be Nils Krogstad not Torvald Helmer
Running that bank.

NORA: That will never happen

KROGSTAD: Well, you're not going / to…

NORA: I do have the courage now.

KROGSTAD: Oh, you don't scare me. A fine spoilt lady
Like you…

NORA: Watch me. Watch me!

KROGSTAD: Under the ice, perhaps?
Down in the cold coal-black water? Bobbing up, in
spring,   bloated   unrecognisable.
Your hair all gone?

NORA: You don't scare me.

KROGSTAD: And you don't scare me. Some things, one
Simply doesn't do, Mrs. Helmer. Besides
What would be the use? I 'd still have your husband
In my pocket.

NORA: After? If I'm…

KROGSTAD: Your reputation lives on. In my hands.

NORA stands speechless.

You have been warned.
So don't do anything stupid. When Helmer's
Read my message, I expect an answer from him.
And you would do well to remember
That it is your husband who has forced me
To do this.
And I'll never forgive him for that.
Goodbye Madam.

He goes out through the hall

NORA goes towards the hall door, opens it a little and listens.

NORA: He's going. He's not going to deliver the letter!
No, that's impossible!

Opens the door more and more.

What is he...? He's standing outside.
Not going down the steps.
He's having second thoughts!
Will he? Is he going to...?

A letter drops into the letterbox.

KROGSTAD's footsteps can be heard disappearing down the steps...

NORA with muffled cry, runs to the sofa table, short pause...

In the letterbox!

Tiptoes shyly over to the hall door.

It's just lying there! Torvald Torvald...now we are beyond
Saving!

MRS LINDE enters with costume from RL.

LINDE: Well, that's as much as I can do. Shall we try
it on...

NORA (*Hoarse, slow.*) Kristine, come here

LINDE throws costume down.

LINDE: What's wrong? You look terrible.

NORA: Come here. See that letter? Look...through the
glass...

LINDE: Yes yes I can see it.

NORA: The letter is from Krogstad.

LINDE: Oh Nora! Krogstad lent you the money!

NORA: Yes. Now Torvald will know everything.

LINDE: Oh Nora it's the best thing. For both of you.

NORA: There's more to it. I forged a signature…

LINDE: For / heavens sake.

NORA: I wish to tell you. You are my witness

LINDE: Witness? / What shall I…

NORA: If I should go mad…and that might happen

LINDE: Nora!

NORA: or if something else happens…something…
　　So I couldn't be here…

LINDE: Nora, Nora…you're crazy!

NORA: If someone tried to take all the blame upon
　　Themselves, all the guilt, you understand?

LINDE: Yes, Yes, but do you / imagine…

NORA: Then you are witness that it isn't true, Kristine.
　　I am absolutely not crazy myself.
　　I am in full control of my senses
　　And I am telling you
　　'Nobody else knew about it
　　I did it all by myself.'
　　Remember that.

LINDE: I will. But I don't understand…

NORA: How could you understand?
　　It is indeed a wonderful thing that's about
　　To happen.

LINDE: A wonderful thing?

NORA: Yes A wonderful thing
    But terrible
    Which mustn't happen not at any price.

LINDE: I'm going to talk to Krogstad. Now!

NORA: Don't. He'll harm you too.

LINDE: There was a time when he would have done
    Anything in the world for me.

NORA: Him.

LINDE: Where does he live?

NORA: How would I know? Oh yes… (*Puts her hand in her pocket.*) …his card
    But the letter…the letter…?

HELMER inside his room, knocks on the door.

HELMER: NORA!

NORA cries in fear.

NORA: What is it? What do you want?

HELMER: Now now! Don't be scared. We're not
    Coming In. You've locked the door.
    Are you trying on your costume?

NORA: Yes! Yes! I am. I'm going to be so lovely,
    Torvald!

LINDE: He lives just round the corner.

NORA: But that's no use! We're lost. The letter
    Is lying in the letter box!

LINDE Your husband has the key?

NORA: Yes.

LINDE: Krogstad must demand his letter back
    Unopened he must think of a reason…

NORA: But usually at this time / Torvald…

LINDE: Delay him. Stop him somehow.
I'll come back as quickly as I can.

She leaves quickly by the hall door.

NORA goes over to HELMER's door peeps in Torvald!

HELMER: (*In the back room.*) Permission to enter one's
Own sitting room? Come on Rank, now we'll see…
What's going on?

NORA: What, dear Torvald?

HELMER: Rank promised me an extraordinary
transformation.

RANK: (*In the doorway.*) Rank jumped the gun.

NORA: Rank did. No-one admires my splendour before
Tomorrow.

HELMER: Dear Nora…you look so anxious
Have you been over-rehearsing?

NORA: No. I haven't rehearsed at all yet.

HELMER: Well, it is necessary…

NORA: Altogether necessary Torvald.
But I need your help. I've forgotten it all.

HELMER: Take it away. We'll soon refresh your memory.

NORA: Yes. Look after me Torvald.
Promise? Oh, I'm so anxious! The big party!
You must sacrifice yourself to me this evening
Torvald. Not a scrap of business not a pen not
A paper in your hand. Yes! Alright? Promise
Me, Torvald?

HELMER: Promise. Entirely at your service. The whole
Evening. Poor little…hmm…actually,
there is one thing I need to do first…

Goes towards the hall door.

NORA: What do you need to do out there?

HELMER: Just see if there are any letters…

NORA: No. No. Absolutely not, Torvald

HELMER: Why?

NORA: You promised. There are no letters.

HELMER: Let me see. Wants to go

NORA, by the piano, plays the first bars of the tarantella…

HELMER: (*By the door stops.*) …Aha…

NORA: I cannot dance tomorrow
If you don't rehearse with me tonight.

HELMER: (*Goes over to her.*) Are you really nervous?

NORA: Yes I'm really nervous
Let me try it now
There's still time before dinner
Sit down and play for me, dear Torvald
Put me right
Guide me like you usually do.

HELMER: With pleasure with great pleasure
At your request.

He sits at piano.

NORA grabs tambourine from the box, plus a long coloured shawls, drapes herself…walks onto the floor…

NORA: Play now for me!
I'll dance now!

HELMER plays and NORA dances.

RANK stands behind HELMER and watches.

HELMER: (*Playing.*) ...Slower...slower...

NORA: I can't.

HELMER: Not so violently. Nora!

NORA: It must be like this.

HELMER: (*Stops.*) No, no this isn't working at all.

NORA laughs, swings her tambourine.

NORA: Wasn't that what I said?

RANK: Let me play for her.

HELMER: (*Gets up.*) Yes do that. Then I can
Give her notes... Guide her...

RANK sits at piano and plays.

NORA dances with increasing wildness.

*HELMER has placed himself by the stove and addresses
instructions to her...she seems not to hear him. Her hair
loosens and falls upon her shoulders. She doesn't notice, but
dances on...*

MRS LINDE enters.

LINDE: Ah!

NORA: Here's some fun, Kristine!

HELMER: Dearest best Nora you're dancing as
If your life depended on it!

NORA: Well it does!

HELMER: Rank! Stop! This is crazy! Stop! Stop it!

RANK stops playing and NORA stops suddenly...

HELMER: (*Over to her.*) I don't believe you.
You've forgotten everything I've taught you.

NORA throws the tambourine away from her.

NORA: I told you.

HELMER: We certainly need some instruction here.

NORA: You see how necessary it is?
　　　You must instruct me to the last detail
　　　Promise me?

HELMER: Trust me.

NORA: You shall not, today or tomorrow
　　　Have thoughts of anything other than me…
　　　No opening letters
　　　No opening letter boxes…

HELMER: Aha…this anxiety is about the man…

NORA: Oh well, him too…

HELMER: Nora I can see it in your face
　　　There is already a letter lying there from him…

NORA: I don't know I think so but you won't
　　　Read such things now. There mustn't be
　　　Anything bad between us until this is over…

RANK: (*Quietly.*) Do as she asks.

HELMER wraps his arms around her…

HELMER: The 'Child' will have her way
　　　But tomorrow night…when you have danced…

NORA: Then you are free.

HELENE is in the doorway to the right.

HELENE: Madam dinner is served.

NORA: We'll have champagne, Helene.

HELENE: Good madam.

Exits.

HELMER: Well well…a great feast then?

NORA: A great feast! Champagne until
The break of day.

Calls out.

And a few macaroons, Helene!
A lot of macaroons, Helene,
Just for once!

HELMER takes her hands.

Now now now…
Enough madness. Now be my own
Recognisable little bird again.

NORA: Yes. I shall. In a moment. Go
In to dinner. You too, Doctor Rank.
Kristine, help me put up my hair…

RANK: (*Quietly, as he goes.*)
There isn't anything…there isn't something on the way?
…is there?

HELMER: Not at all. Nothing but these Performance
Jitters…
They go in to the right…

NORA: Well????

LINDE: He's gone to the country.

NORA: I read your face.

LINDE: He's coming back tomorrow evening.
I left him a note.

NORA: You should have just let it go. You can't stop it.
And…in the end…it's a joy
This here waiting for the wonderful thing.

LINDE: So why are you waiting?

NORA: You couldn't possibly understand. Go in to the
others.
I'll come in a second…

MRS LINDE goes into the dinner.

NORA stands a while then she looks at her watch.

NORA: Five.
Seven hours to midnight.
Then twenty four hours to the midnight after that.
Then the tarantella will be over.
Twenty four and…seven…?
Thirty one hours to live.

HELMER: (*In the doorway to the right.*) What's happened to
That little bird?

NORA: (*Towards him, with open arms.*) That little bird?
She's flying to you!

End of Act Two.

ACT THREE

The day after Christmas

The same room. The sofa table, with chairs around it is in the middle of the floor. A lamp burns on the table. Door to the hall stands open. Dance music comes from the floor above. MRS LINDE sits by the table leafing distractedly through a book. A couple of times she listens at the door.

LINDE: (*Looking at her watch.*) Still not here! It's high time he!

If only he doesn't...listens again... Oh, here he is!

She goes out to the hall, carefully opens the outer door. Quiet footsteps up the stairs.

(*Whispers.*) Come in. There's no one here.

KROGSTAD: (*Doorway.*) I got your note. What's it mean?

LINDE: I must talk to you.

KROGSTAD: Must you? And it must be here?

LINDE: My place is impossible. There's no private Entrance to my room. Come in. We're all alone. The Maid's gone to bed and the Helmers are Upstairs at the ball...

KROGSTAD: (*Enters.*) Well, well, the Helmers are dancing this Evening!

LINDE: Why not?

KROGSTAD: Why not indeed?

LINDE: Krogstad we should talk...

KROGSTAD: Have we anything left to say to one another?

LINDE: We have a lot to say to one another.

KROGSTAD: I don't think so.

LINDE: No…because you never ever understood me.

KROGSTAD: What was there to understand? The simplest
Lesson. Better Offer!
Heartless Woman Gives Man
Marching Orders.

LINDE: Do you really think I'm heartless?
Do you really think I left you without any
Damage in here?

KROGSTAD: Didn't you?

LINDE: Nils how can you believe that?

KROGSTAD: If it wasn't like that why did you write what
you did?

LINDE: I had to. If I was breaking from you…I had to…it
was
My duty to…exterminate all your feelings about me.

KROGSTAD: So that's why. And…all just for money!

LINDE: I had a helpless mother and two little fatherless
brothers!
We couldn't wait for you, Krogstad!
Your 'prospects 'couldn't help us!

KROGSTAD: I know. But you had no right to reject me for
Someone else.

LINDE: No. Yes. Actually
I ask myself all the time if I had that right?

KROGSTAD: (*More quietly.*) When I lost you all the firm
earth

Under my feet   vanished   look at me
I'm a castaway   on a wreck   of a career.

LINDE: Help could be on its way.

KROGSTAD: It was on its way then you came along
stood in its path!

LINDE: Without knowing that Krogstad!
I only knew today that I was replacing you…

KROGSTAD: If you say so, I believe you. But now you
know…
Clear the Way…

LINDE: No. It wouldn't help.

KROGSTAD: It would ! Try it.

LINDE: I've learned to act sensibly. Life and
Bitter necessity were my very good teachers.

KROGSTAD: And life has taught me very well Don't
believe
In just 'Words'.

LINDE: Then life has been a sensible teacher. But you still
Believe in Actions?

KROGSTAD: What do you mean?

LINDE: You're a castaway on a wreck.

KROGSTAD: Yes

LINDE: I'm a castaway too   on a desert island of a Life
No survivors no Man Friday.

KROGSTAD: Your decision.

LINDE: The only possible decision.

KROGSTAD: Well. So?

LINDE: Nils   suppose two castaways held out
    Their hands…

KROGSTAD: What are you saying?

LINDE: Two   even on a desert island   stand a better
    chance
    Of survival   than one   on a wreck. All at sea
    Crying…help?

KROGSTAD: Kristine!

LINDE: Why did you think I came to town?

KROGSTAD: You had a thought or two about me?

LINDE: I must work or I go mad. All my life, always,
    I've worked and it's been my best my only
    Pleasure. But now, I'm all alone in the world
    And it's terrible. I'm empty and forsaken
    There's no joy in working for yourself
    Krogstad provide me with someone and
    Something to work for!

KROGSTAD: I don't believe this. This is Romantic Fiction!
    Woman Sacrifices Herself!

LINDE: Krogstad. Romantic. Me????

KROGSTAD: You really mean it? You recall my past?

LINDE: Yes.

KROGSTAD: And my present reputation?

LINDE: I thought you once said with me you
    Could be different.

KROGSTAD: And oh I meant it.

LINDE: Then you still can.

KROGSTAD: Kristine you're saying all this after
    The Most Careful Consideration…? Yes you are…
    I can see you…have you really got the courage…

LINDE: I need someone to be a mother for
    And your children need a mother
    We two Robinson Crusoes need each other
    Krogstad Let's find some solid ground
    And walk.

KROGSTAD: grasps her hands Thank you thank you
    Kristine!
    Now shall I also save myself in other people's
    Eyes? Oh, but I forgot…

LINDE: (*Listens.*) Shhh The tarantella! Go on

KROGSTAD: Why? What is it?

LINDE: Do you hear that music? When it stops…
    We can expect them.

KROGSTAD: All right, I'll go. But its all in vain!
    You don't know what I have done to the Helmers…

LINDE: Yes, I do.

KROGSTAD: And still you're brave / enough to…

LINDE: I understand despair and how it drives you / to…

KROGSTAD: Oh if only I could undo this?

LINDE: But you can. Your letter is lying in the letter
    Box still.

KROGSTAD: Are you sure?

LINDE: Absolutely sure.

KROGSTAD: (*Looks searchingly at her.*) Is this what it's all
    About? To save your friend whatever the cost?
    Tell me is it?

LINDE: Krogstad. A woman who once sold herself for
    Others, doesn't do it again.

KROGSTAD: I will demand my letter back.

LINDE: No No.

KROGSTAD: Oh Yes I'll stay here until Helmer comes
down…
Say to him 'Give me my letter back, there's a
Good Chap. Only concerns my dismissal…
No need to Read, Old Boy'.

LINDE: No, Nils, you wont demand your letter back.

KROGSTAD: Wasn't that why you got me here?

LINDE: Yes initially in my mad panic but
I'm a day older now and I've seen
Extraordinary events during that time
Right here in this house Helmer must
Learn everything. This poisonous secret
Must be exposed there must be a full
Understanding between those two
That can't happen with all this concealing
And evading…

KROGSTAD: Well…if you dare…there's one thing I can
do…
And do now!

LINDE: listens Hurry. Go go! The dance is finishing…
We're not safe here…

KROGSTAD: I'll wait for you outside.

LINDE: Yes. Do that. Then you can walk me home.

KROGSTAD: I've never ever before been so unbelievably
happy!

*He goes out through the outer door. The door between sitting
room and hall remains open…*

*MRS LINDE tidies up a little. Gets her outdoor things ready
as…*

LINDE: What a change! Yes what a change!

People to work for to live for a home to
…bring warmth into! Now things will start to /
…mesh… I hope they will come. Aha here they
Are. Clothes on.

She takes her hat and coat.

HELMER's and NORA's voices are heard outside.

A key is turned.

*HELMER leads NORA almost forcibly into the hall. She is
dressed in the Italian costume with a large black shawl over
it. He is in evening dress with an open black domino on top.*

NORA is in the doorway, reluctant…both somewhat tiddly…

NORA: No, no, not in here! I want to go upstairs again!
I don't want to leave so early!

HELMER: But dearest Nora…

NORA: Oh I'm asking you so imploringly, Torvald!
So deeply   beautifully…just one hour more!

HELMER: Not one minute more, my sweet Nora. An
Agreement is an agreement. Into the sitting room!
Here, you're catching a chill…

He leads her gently, her resisting, into the room…

LINDE: Good evening

NORA: Kristine!

HELMER: Mrs Linde…here so late!

LINDE: Yes I'm sorry I so wanted to see Nora All
Dressed Up!

NORA: Have you been sitting here waiting for me?

LINDE: Yes. I was late you were upstairs
Then I thought… 'Kristine you must wait and see her'

HELMER: (*Taking off NORA's shawl.*) …Of course you must.
Look! Now…is that worth the wait? Isn't
She delightful, Mrs Linde?

LINDE: Oh, I must say!

HELMER: Is she not remarkably delightful?
That was the Majority Verdict of The Party!
But she is terribly stubborn the sweet little thing
What are we to do?
I practically had to use Brute Strength to
Get her to leave!

NORA: Oh Torvald you'll rue the day you didn't
Indulge me one half hour longer…you'll
Rue / the day…

HELMER: Listen to it, madam. She dances her tarantella…
Thundering Success Very Well Deserved…
Although, in the performance, perhaps rather too
Much naturalness I think in my opinion
A little more strictly speaking than is required by
The Demands Of art! But that's By the By! The
Main Point is…she was a success a thundering
Success. Should I let her stay after that? Weaken
The Effect? No thank you! I took my delightful
Capri girl – capricious Capri girl you might say –
Under My Wing…a quick sweep of the ballroom…
Bowing to All Sides…and…as it says in Romantic
Novels…The Vision Of Beauty Melted Away.
An exit should always effect, Mrs Linde, but could I
Make Nora understand…? Phoo…it's hot in here

He throws his domino on a chair and opens the door to his room.

What? It is dark in there. Oh yes; of course.
Excuse me.

He goes in and lights a couple of candles.

NORA whispers quickly, breathlessly.

NORA: Well?

LINDE: I've spoken to him.

NORA: And…?

LINDE: Nora…you must tell your husband everything.

NORA: I knew it.

LINDE: You've absolutely nothing to fear from Krogstad.
But you must tell him all the same.

NORA: I won't.

LINDE: Then the letter will.

NORA: Thank you Kristine. Now I know what I have
To do…shhh…

HELMER: (*Returning.*) Now madam, finished admiring her?

LINDE: Yes and now I'll say goodnight.

HELMER: Oh, already? Is this yours…the knitting?

LINDE: takes it Yes thank you I nearly forgot it.

HELMER: You knit then?

LINDE: Yes?

HELMER: Little tip try embroidery instead.

LINDE: Oh why?

HELMER: It looks far more beautiful Look
One holds the embroidery thus with the left
Hand…then one plies the needle with the right
Hand thus in a long elegant parabola…see?

LINDE: Yes / …that's as.

HELMER: Whereas knitting on the other hand…just
Looks ugly – knitting needles going up and down…

It's got something Chinese about it! That was
An excellent champagne they served!

LINDE: Yes. Good night, Nora. Don't be stubborn any
more.

HELMER: Well said, Mrs Linde!

LINDE: Good night, Mr Director.

HELMER follows her to the door.

HELMER: Good night good night! I hope you'll get home
safe?
It would be my pleasure to…but you don't have such
A very long walk have you? Good night, good night.

She goes.

He closes the door after her and comes in again.

Well, Finally! We finally got her out the door!
She's a crashing bore, that woman.

NORA: Aren't you very tired, Torvald?

HELMER: No, not at all.

NORA: Not sleepy?

HELMER: Absolutely not. On the contrary…I feel
Tremendously exhilarated!
What about you? Yes you certainly look tired
and sleepy.

NORA: Yes, I am very tired. I want to sleep.

HELMER; You see you see! I was right not to let you stay
Any longer.

NORA: Oh Everything you do is right.

HELMER: (*Kisses her on her forehead.*) Now the exotic
Parrot speaks like a human! Did you notice how
Cheerful Rank was this evening?

NORA: Oh? Was He? I didn't get to speak to him.

HELMER: Neither did I very much. But I haven't seen him
In such spirits for ages.

He looks at her for a time, then comes nearer to her.

Mmm. It's delightful to come home and be
Oneself, quite alone with you – oh you
Fascinating young woman!

NORA: Don't look at me like that, Torvald.

HELMER: Not look at my most treasured possession?
At all the magnificence which is mine, mine
Alone totally utterly?

NORA: (*Goes over to the other side of the table.*) Don't
Speak to me like that tonight.

HELMER: (*Follows her.*) I see the tarantella still coursing
Through your veins. Which makes you more
Attractive. Listen…the guests are starting to leave
Nora soon the whole house will be silent.

NORA: I hope so.

HELMER: Yes of course you do. My own beloved Nora.
Do you know when I'm with you at a party…why
I speak so little to you…stay away from you…
Send a stolen glance now and then do you know
Why I do that? I'm pretending you're my secret
Beloved my young secret fiancee and no-one at
The party has any idea at all that there is something
Between us…

NORA: Oh yes yes I know that you're always thinking
About me.

HELMER: And then, when its time to go and I lay your
shawl
About your slender youthful shoulders

the wonderful curve of your neck   I imagine you're
My bride   that we've just come from the wedding
Feast   that for the first time I'm leading you
Into my house   that for the first time I'm alone
With you quite alone   with your young trembling
Loveliness. All this evening I've been longing for
You. When I saw you *prowl* and *tease* in
Your tarantella my blood *boiled.* I couldn't wait.
That's why I made you leave so early.

NORA: Stop it, Torvald. You must leave me alone. I don't
Want this.

HELMER: What does that mean? You're being a fluttering
Bird again, aren't you, little Nora? Want?
Want? Am I not your husband?

There is a knock at the door.

NORA starts.

Did you hear?

(*Towards the hall.*) Who is it?

RANK: (*Outside.*) It's me. Dare I come in for a moment?

HELMER: (*Quietly annoyed.*) What does he want now?
Aloud.
Just a second.

Opens the door.

How kind of you not
To walk right past our door.

RANK: I thought I heard your voice and then I
so much wanted to drop in.
lets his eyes wander around...
Yes yes Dear dear familiar room. You have it so
Warm and cosy, you two.

HELMER: You seemed to be enjoying yourself upstairs.

RANK: Enormously. Why not? Why not take everything
  The world offers? As much as one can for as
  Long as one can! The wine / was splendid.

HELMER: The champagne in particular.

RANK: You thought so too? Its unbelievable how
  Much I was able to wash down.

NORA: Torvald drank a lot of champagne this evening too.

RANK: Did he?

NORA: Yes and then he's always so amusing afterwards.

RANK: Well why shouldn't you award yourself a
  Happy evening after a good day's work?

HELMER: A good day's work? Unfortunately, I couldn't
  Claim to have done that today...

RANK: (*Claps him on the shoulder.*) Ah, but I can!

NORA: Dr Rank, surely you were undertaking a
  Scientific examination today, weren't you?

RANK: Yes I was.

HELMER: Look look! Little Nora discussing a
  Scientific examination!

NORA: And dare I congratulate you on the outcome?

RANK: You dare.

NORA: It was good then?

RANK: The best possible for both doctor and patient.
  Certainty.

NORA: (*Urgently.*) Certainty?

RANK: Absolute certainty. Didn't I deserve a happy
  Evening after that?

NORA: Yes, you did, Dr Rank.

HELMER: I agree. As long as you don't have to pay
For it tomorrow.

RANK: In this life you don't get anything for nothing.

NORA: Doctor Rank you're fond of masked balls aren't
you?

RANK: Yes…when there are lots of hilarious disguises.

NORA: Listen what shall we two be at the next masked
ball?

HELMER: Miss forever Frivolous already
thinking about the next one?

RANK: We two? Yes I'll tell you
You'll be Fortune's Child.

HELMER: Yes but find the costume that / depicts that…

RANK: Let your wife wear what she wants
as she walks through the world.

HELMER: Splendidly said. And do you have any idea
What you'll be going as?

RANK: Oh yes. The clearest idea.

HELMER: Well?

RANK: At the next masked ball I'll be invisible.

HELMER: Now there's an idea!

RANK: There's a very large black hat…have you
Never heard of The Invisibility Hat?
You pull it right over your head.
And then no-one can see you any more.

HELMER: (*Suppressed smile.*) No-one at all.

RANK: I've forgotten why I came. Helmer, give me
A cigar, one of those dark Havanas.

HELMER: (*Pleasure.*) Offers the case.

RANK: (*Takes one, cuts off the end.*) Thank you.

NORA strikes a match.

NORA: Let me give you a light.

RANK: Thank you.

She holds the match for him.

He lights the cigar.

And so farewell?

HELMER: Farewell, farewell dear friend!

NORA: Sleep well, Doctor Rank.

RANK: Thank you for the wish.

NORA: Wish me the same.

RANK: You? Well…since you wish it… Sleep well.
And thank you for the light.

He nods to both of them and goes.

HELMER: (*Undertone.*) Drunk.

NORA: Maybe so.

HELMER takes his keys and goes into the hall.

Torvald…what are you doing out there?

HELMER: Emptying the letter box. It's quite full.
there'll be no room for the papers tomorrow
Morning…

NORA: Are you going to work tonight?

HELMER: You know very well I don't want to… What's
This? Someone's been at the lock!

NORA: At the lock?

HELMER: Yes! What's going on? I wouldn't have thought
The servants…there's a broken hairpin here…
Nora, it's one of yours…

NORA: Then it must have been the children…

HELMER: Then you really must stop them ! Hmm hmm…
There…got it open anyway.

Takes out contents, calls out to the kitchen.

Helene! Helene, put out the porch light.

*He comes in again and closes the door to the hall with the
letters in his hand.*

See! How they've piled up? (*Leafs through.*) What's this?

NORA: (*By the window.*) The letter! Oh no, no, Torvald!

HELMER: Two visiting cards from Rank.

NORA: From Doctor Rank?

HELMER: (*Looks at them.*) Doctor of Medicine Rank. They
Were lying on top he must have put them in
When he left.

NORA: Is there anything on them?

HELMER: There's a black cross over the name. Look.
That's a bit ghoulish, isn't it? Like he's giving
Notification of his death…

NORA: He is.

HELMER: What? Do you know about it? Has he said
something?

NORA: Yes. When the cards come, he's taken leave
Of us. He's going to lock himself away and die.

HELMER: My poor friend. I knew I wouldn't have him
For long…but so soon…and then he hides himself
Away like a wounded animal.

NORA: When it happens, it's better it happens
Wordlessly. Isn't that right, Torvald?

HELMER: (*Walks up and down.*) He's such a part of us.
I don't think I can imagine him gone!
He with his pains and his loneliness
Was the cloud background of our sunlit
Happiness …well perhaps all for the best.
For us too, Nora. Now we are left to
Just each other.

Puts his arms round her.

Oh my beloved wife!
I don't think I can hold you tightly enough!
Do you know Nora…so often I wish
Some terrible danger would threaten you…
Just so that I can risk life limb, everything
Just for you.

NORA tears herself away strongly and firmly.

Now you must read your letters Torvald.

HELMER: No no, not tonight. Tonight I want to be with
my wife.

NORA: Your friend is dying.

HELMER: Yes. This has shaken us both. Ugliness and
thoughts about death   decay has come between us.
We must free ourselves of it.
Until then…let's each go to our own room…

NORA: (*Arms round his neck.*) Torvald…Good night, good
night!

HELMER kisses her forehead.

Good night you my little songbird.
Sleep well, Nora. Now…letters…

He takes the bundle into his room and closes the door behind him.

NORA, wild eyed, grasps HELMER's domino, wraps it round herself…

Never to see him again.
Never. Never. Never.

Throws her shawl over her head.

Never to see the children again either. Not in
Eternity. Never. Never.
Oh the ice-cold black water Oh the bottomless…
this…oh if it was only over
Now he has it now he's reading it
Oh no, not yet Torvald goodbye to you and
The children…

She is about to rush into the hall.

Then HELMER tears his door open and stands there with the opened letter in his hand.

HELMER: Nor / a!

NORA: Ah!

HELMER: What's this? Do you know what this / letter
says?

NORA: Yes I know. Let me go! / Let me get out!

HELMER holds her back.

HELMER: Where are you going?

NORA tries to tear herself free.

NORA: You shan't save me, / Torvald!

HELMER: Is it true? What he writes? Terrible! No, no
It's impossible / that it's true.

NORA: It is true. I've loved you more than
Anything in the whole world.

HELMER: Don't come here with your / stupid phrases.

NORA: Torvald...

HELMER: You... Disaster!
/ Do you know what you've done?

NORA: Let me go. You'll not take the blame. You
Shall not take it upon yourself.

HELMER: No more melodramatics!

Locks the hall door.

You're going to stay and give an account
Of yourself!
Do you understand what you've done?
Do you?

NORA looks at him intently, her expression stiffens.

NORA: Yes, now I am beginning
to understand it length and breadth

HELMER: (*Walks about the floor.*) Well this is a rude
awakening!
In all these eight years she who was my pride and
Joy...a hypocrite and liar...no...worse!
A criminal! Oh the fathomless bottomless ugliness
Of it! Shame on you shame on you!

NORA keeps looking intently at him.

I should have known something like this would
happen! I should have foreseen it!
Inherited all your father's wobbling principles!

Be quiet! All your father's wobbly dubious morals!
No religion, no morals, no sense of duty…oh how
I'm being punished for turning a blind eye
To his character. I did it to win you…
And this is how you repay me.

NORA: Yes this is how.

HELMER: You've destroyed my whole happiness.
Ruined all my future. Oh it doesn't bear
thinking about! I am at the mercy of a
Totally unscrupulous man he can do with
Me what he wants! Demand anything of me!
Order me about command me at will! And
I can't say One Word! And to have to sink so
Wretchedly because of a silly silly woman!

NORA: When I'm gone, you'll be free.

HELMER: Spare me the gestures! These are the
Empty Phrases your father always dealt out.
What use would it be to me if you were gone?
Not the slightest use! He could still tell the
World everything!…if he does everybody will suspect
I knew all about your criminal behaviour.!
They'll think I stood behind you…
Guiding you. Urging you on! And this is what
I can thank you for…you who I've carried in
My hands all through our whole marriage.
Do you understand what you've done to me?

NORA: (*Cold, calm.*) Yes.

HELMER: It's so unbelievable I can hardly get a grip on it
But we must put it right. Take off your shawl.
Take. It. Off! I must appease him one way
Or another. Its got to be hushed up…whatever
The cost! And where We are concerned…it must
Look as if everything's normal.

But of course, only to Outside Eyes.
You'll stay here that goes without saying
But I'm not having you raising my children
I daren't let you. I have to say this to
Her whom I loved so deeply and still...
Now that's enough It's over. After today
Happiness is not an option. It's a matter of...
Picking up the pieces...assembling them into
A...

The porch bell rings.

HELMER starts.

What's that? So late!
Should the most dreadful thing...
should he? Nora! Say you are ill /

NORA remains motionless.

HELMER goes and opens the hall door.

HELENE half dressed in the hall door.

HELENE: A letter has come for Madam.

HELMER: Give it to me. (*Grabs the letter, closes the door.*)
Yes, from him. You're not getting it. I'll read it.

NORA: Yes. You read it.

HELMER: (*By the lamp.*) I haven't the courage...perhaps
We are lost you and I, Nora. No. I need to...

Breaks open the letter. Reads the accompanying paper. A cry.

Nora!

NORA looks at him.

Nora! Let me reread it. Yes yes yes...I am safe!
Nora! I'm safe!

NORA: And I?

HELMER: You too of course! We're both safe both of us.
Look   He's returned your promissory note. He writes
He's sorry and regrets…that a happy upturn in
His life…oh it is the same as I read…We are
Saved, Nora! No-one can harm you at all!
Oh Nora, Nora, no let's get rid of all this
Ugly stuff…let me see… (*Looks at writing.*)
No I don't want to see it…it's all now just
A bad dream.

Tears it up, throws it in stove…watches as it burns.

There. Gone. An ex-letter. He wrote that
Christmas eve…oh, what a terrible three days
For you, Nora…

NORA: Yes, I've fought a terrible battle these past
Three days.

HELMER: And upset yourself…not seeing any way out
other
Than… No, let's not bring up this hideousness!
We can only celebrate and repeat 'it is over it
Is over! Listen to me, Nora! You don't seem
To realise… It is over. What's this then –
This long face? Oh poor little thing…I
Understand…you can't believe I've forgiven you!
But I have! Nora, I promise you I've
Forgiven you everything. What you did, I
Know you did out of love for me.

NORA: That's true

HELMER: You've loved me as a wife should love a
Husband. It was just you couldn't possibly
Have the insight to judge your actions. But
Do you think that makes you less dear to me
…that on your own you get things wrong?
No, no just lean on me I'll advise you I'll
Guide you. I wouldn't be a man if this lovely

Helplessness didn't make you twice as
Lovely to me. I forbid you to remember
Any of my hard words. They were just
Dread when I felt everything was
Coming crashing down on my head! I
Have forgiven you, Nora, I promise
I have forgiven you.

NORA: Thank you for your forgiveness.

She goes out through the door on the right.

HELMER: No stay. (*He looks in.*) What are you doing
In there?

NORA: (*Inside.*) Taking off my masquerade costume.

HELMER: (*In the doorway.*) Yes, do that. Poor little bird…
fly home safely. Let's smooth disturbed feathers.
Home to roost. I've got broad wings to cover you
With (*Walks about beside the door.*) Oh how warm
And cosy our nest is, Nora. A bird sanctuary. I've
Got you safe homing pigeon, safe from that hawk's
Talons. I'll rest your little beating heart. Little by
Little. Trust me, Nora. By tomorrow, everything
Will look different…everything will be back to
Normal. I wont have to keep on saying 'I pardon
You' you'll feel released. How can you possibly
Think I'd prosecute you or arraign you at all? Ever?
You cannot understand a real man's true heart.
Nora. For a man there's something so sweet
so satisfying about knowing him knowing he's
Forgiven his wife forgiven her with his whole
Heart. Its as if she becomes his even more. It's
As if he brings her into the world again, like his
child. From now on…that's what you are for me…
Torvald's Girl Child…Born at Christmas! No more
Worries, Nora. Just openness I am your Will
And your Conscience. What's… Not bound for bed?
You've changed?

NORA: (*In her day clothes.*) Yes, Torvald, I've changed.

HELMER: But why? Now? It's so late…

NORA: I'm not sleeping tonight.

HELMER: Nora! Dear…

NORA: (*Looks at watch.*) It's not that late. Sit yourself here, Torvald. We two have a lot to talk about.

She sits down at one side of the table.

HELMER: Nora! Now what's this! The long face again…

NORA: Sit yourself down. This will take a long time.
I've so much to say to you.

HELMER sits across the table from her.

HELMER: You're worrying me, Nora…I don't understand /
you…

NORA: No, that's just it. You don't understand me. And
I've never understood you either until this evening
You must listen to what I say. This is an Appeal,
Torvald.

HELMER: What do you mean?

NORA: (*Short pause.*) See how we sit? Does anything strike
You?

HELMER: What?

NORA: We've been married for eight years. Doesn't it
Strike you that this is the first time we two
You and I man and wife have sat down for
A serious talk?

HELMER: What do you mean serious?

NORA: For eight whole years…no longer…right from
The day we met…we've never exchanged one
serious word about one serious thing.

HELMER: You're saying I should have bothered you with
all my worries you couldn't possibly have
Helped me with?

NORA: I'm not talking about worries. I'm saying we
Never once sat down seriously together and
Tried to get to the bottom of anything!

HELMER: But dearest Nora, Would good would it have
Done you if we had?

NORA: And there we have the heart of the matter.
You've never understood me. Such injustice
Has been practised against me. First by Pappa
Then by you.

HELMER: What? The two of us loved you more than
Anything else in the world!

NORA: (*Shakes her head.*) You've never loved me.
You just loved being in love with me.

HELMER: Nora its not true!

NORA: It is true, Torvald. When I lived at home with
Pappa, he dished out his opinions
and they became my opinions
Any others one's he didn't like I hid
He called me his doll child and he played
With me as I played with my dolls…
And when I came here to your house…

HELMER: Nice description of our wedding!

NORA: I mean I passed from Pappa's hands to yours.
You arranged everything to your tastes…
Those tastes became mine or I pretended they did
I really don't know…probably both…sometimes one
Sometimes the other…When I look at it now…
I think I've lived here like a beggar
from hand to mouth   I've lived by doing tricks for you,

Torvald.
And that's how you liked it. You and Pappa
Have committed a criminal act against me.
I have become nothing and You are guilty.

HELMER: Nora! How unreasonable and ungrateful!
Haven't you been happy?

NORA: No, never. I thought I was. But I never have been.

HELMER: Not...not happy?

NORA: No just cheerful. And you've always been so kind
To me. But our house has never been anything but a
Playroom. I've been your doll-wife just as I was
Pappa's doll-child. And my children I've made
Them my dolls in their turn. I thought it was fun
When you played games with me just as I thought
It was fun when I played with them. That has
Been our marriage, Torvald.

HELMER: There's something true in this...a bit
exaggerated
A bit overwrought I think but...from now on...it
Will be different. Playtime is over. Time for
School!

NORA: Whose school? Mine or the children's?

HELMER: Yours and the children's, darling Nora.

NORA: Oh Torvald you are not the man to teach me
How to be the right wife for you.

HELMER: How can you say that?

NORA: And I...what school did I go to to learn
What to teach children?

HELMER: Nora!

NORA: ...you said it yourself just now...you
Daren't trust me with that job...

HELMER: in the heat of the moment! You mustn't take /
any
Notice of that!

NORA: But you were right. I'm not qualified. There's
Something to sort out first. I have to educate
Myself. And you're not the right man for the job.
But I'm the right woman. And that's why I'm
Leaving you now.

HELMER: (*Jumping to his feet.*) What did you say?

NORA: I must stand alone if I'm to understand myself
And everything out there. That's why I can't
Stay here any longer.

HELMER: Nora! Nora!

NORA: I need to go now. Kristine will put me up
For tonight

HELMER: You are out of your mind! You don't get
Permission! I forbid it.

NORA: Its no use forbidding me. I don't need
Permission any more. I'll take what belongs
To me. I don't want anything from you,
Now or ever.

HELMER: This is Insanity!

NORA: Tomorrow I'll go home…I mean
the place I came from…
that's the place to start from…

HELMER: Oh you blind, inexperienced creature

NORA: Then the creature must get experience, Torvald
So she can see…

HELMER: Leave your home? Your husband? Your
children?
Think what people will say!

NORA: I can't think about them. I can only think what's
Necessary for me.

HELMER: Oh this is outrageous! You are betraying
Your holiest duties!

NORA: What in your opinion are those?

HELMER: You know what! To your
Husband! To your children!

NORA: I've other equally holy duties.

HELMER: No you haven't! What?

NORA: My duties to myself.

HELMER: You are first! Foremost! A wife and
Mother!

NORA: I don't believe that any more.
I think I am first and foremost a human being
Just as much a one as you are
Or at least I'm trying to become one
I know most people and most books too
Will say you are right, Torvald
But what most people and most books say
…I can't let them guide me any more
I must think for myself
I must understand for myself.

HELMER: Then try to understand your position
Viz-a-vis your own home!
There's an infallible guide in such
Circumstances. Its called Your Religion.

NORA: Oh Torvald. I really don't know what
My religion is.

HELMER: What are you saying now?

NORA: I don't know anything more than Pastor
Hansen passed on at my confirmation!

He said religion is this and is that.
When I leave all this and I'm on my own
I'll examine this matter too.
I'll see if what Pastor Hansen said
Is right or if it is right for me.

HELMER: Young women like you don't do this!
Listen if religion isn't going to be your guide...
Let's appeal to your conscience! You still
Have a moral sense? Have you? Perhaps that's
Left too!

NORA: Well, Torvald that's hard. I really don't know.
I am in complete confusion about that. I only know
...my opinion is the polar opposite of yours
I've discovered this Christmas that the law is
Not what I thought...and I can't accept that
The law is right. If a woman cannot spare
Her old dying father...or save her husband's
Life...that can't be right.

HELMER: You're talking like a child.
You don't understand the society / we live in.

NORA: No, I don't. But now I'm entering into it.
I'll see who's right It or Me.

HELMER: You're sick. You're Fevered. I think you're
Out of your senses.

NORA: I've never felt so clear and certain as tonight.

HELMER: You're clear and certain and abandoning your
Husband and children?

NORA: Yes I am.

HELMER: Then there's only one possible explanation.

NORA: What's that?

HELMER: You don't love me any more.

NORA: That's exactly it.

HELMER: Nora! And you can just say it!

NORA: Oh it hurts me so much for you've always
   been so kind to me
   But there's nothing I can do
   I don't love you any more.

HELMER: (*Fights for calm.*) Is this also clear and certain?

NORA: Completely. That is why I can't stay here any more.

HELMER: Can you explain to me how I've lost your love?

NORA: I've waited so patiently. Eight years! God knows
   I know that the wonderful doesn't happen every day
   Then this shattering thing happened
   And I was completely certain…the wonderful is
   Coming…while Krogstad's letter was lying out there
   It never occurred to me for a second that
   You'd give in to his conditions.
   I was clear and certain you would say to him
   'Tell the whole world if you like'
   And after that.

HELMER: And after that…after I'd exposed my wife
   To shame and disgrace.

NORA: After that I was clear and certain you would
   Step forward and take everything upon yourself
   And say 'I'm the guilty one'.

HELMER: Nora…

NORA: You think I would never have let you sacrifice
   Yourself? That goes without saying. But how
   Would my words have counted against yours?
   That was the wonderful thing I went and hoped for…
   And to stop that thing happening, I wanted to end my
   life!

HELMER: I'd gladly work for you day and night, Nora.
For your sake I'd endure any grief any
hardship…
But no man sacrifices his honour for the
One he loves.

NORA: Hundreds of thousands of women have.

HELMER: You're still thinking and speaking
like a senseless child.

NORA: I accept that. But you still not speaking
Or thinking like a man I can share my life with.
When you stopped being frightened
At the threat to you not me
When all danger passed…for you…
It was as if nothing had happened.
I was still your little bird your doll
Which hereafter was so fragile and delicate…
You had to carry it twice as carefully…

She gets up.

That's the moment I
Realised I've been living for eight years
With a stranger and had three children
With him…I can't bear to think of it!
It rips me to pieces.

HELMER: Heavily I see now. I see.
There's an abyss between us.
Oh but Nora…can't we close it?

NORA: As I am now, I'm no wife for you.

HELMER: I can become a different husband.

NORA: Perhaps. If the doll is taken from you.

HELMER: To be divorced from you ! Divorced!
No no Nora, I can't entertain that thought!

NORA goes to the right.

NORA: All the more reason to do it.

She comes back with her outdoor clothes and a small travel bag, which she puts on the chair by the table.

HELMER: Nora Nora not now. Wait until tomorrow.

NORA: (*Donning her coat.*) I can't spend a night in a
Strange man's room.

HELMER: Then can't we live here like brother and sister?

NORA: (*Puts on her hat.*) You know very well how long
That would last… (*Wraps the shawl round her.*)
Goodbye Torvald. I wont look in on the
Little ones. I know they're in better hands
Than mine. How I am now, I can be nothing to them.

HELMER: But one day Nora…one day…?

NORA: How can I know? I don't even know what will
Happen to me.

HELMER: But you're my wife as you are and as you will be.

NORA: Listen Torvald
when a wife walks out of her husband's
House as I do now I hear according to law
He's released from all his obligations towards her
Anyway
I hereby release you from all your obligations.
You must not feel bound by anything
And nor must I.
Look here's your ring
Give me mine.

HELMER: This too?

NORA: This too.

HELMER: Here.

NORA: So. Now. It's over. I'm putting my keys here
  Concerning house things…ask the maids …they
  Know better than me. Tomorrow when I've gone
  Kristine will come for the things I brought with
  Me here. I'd like them sent on to me.

HELMER: Over! Over? Nora will you ever think of me?

NORA: Of course often you and the children and
  The house.

HELMER: Let me write / to you.

NORA: No never Permission Denied.

HELMER: But I must send /

NORA: Nothing / nothing.

HELMER: …help if you need it…

NORA: No. To repeat. I accept nothing from strangers.

HELMER: Nora…can I never be anything but a stranger
  to you?

  NORA takes her travel bag.

NORA: Oh Torvald…only if the most wonderful thing were
  To happen…

HELMER: Tell me what this most wonderful thing is!

NORA: This. Both you and I would have to change
  So much…that…Oh, Torvald…I no longer
  Believe in anything wonderful.

HELMER: But I will! Tell me. Change ourselves so that…?

NORA: That our life together could become a marriage.
  Goodbye.

  She goes out through the hall.

HELMER sinks down on a chair by the door and covers his face with his hands.

HELMER: Nora! Nora!

He looks round and gets up.

Empty. She's not here any more.

A hope leaps.

The most wonderful thing?!

From below the clang of a gate slamming shut.

The End.